A Critique of Mau: *Mute Compulsion* and Other Essays
Seven More Argumentative Essays

AF211810

Ib Gram-Jensen

A Critique of Mau: *Mute Compulsion* and Other Essays

Seven More Argumentative Essays

© 2023 Ib Gram-Jensen
Publisher: BoD – Books on Demand, Hellerup, Denmark
Press: BoD – Books on Demand, Norderstedt, Germany
ISBN: 978-87-4304-503-8

For Susanne

Contents

Introduction   p. 9
1. A Critique of Mau: *Mute Compulsion*   p. 13
2. A Critical Comment on Meiksins Wood:
"History or Technological Determinism?"   p. 31
3. Comments on Hindess & Hirst:
Pre-Capitalist Modes of Production   p. 75
4. Human Agency   p. 129
5. In Defence of *Structure, Agency and Theory*   p. 151
6. On *Experience and Historical Materialism*   p. 177
7. Once Again, the Problem of Reading Marx   p. 199
References   p. 211

Introduction.

The three first of the seven essays in this book are critiques of Søren Mau's *Mute Compulsion*, Ellen Meiksins Wood's essay "History or Technological Determinism" in her book *Democracy Against Capitalism* and Barry Hindess & Paul Q. Hirst's *Pre-capitalist Modes of Production* respectively. The two first-mentioned are criticised for giving a misleading account of Marx' (and Engels') historical materialism, more precisely for the failure to recognise the conception of the dialectic of forces and relations of production as the motive power of historical development and transformations as a core element in that historical materialism, and the expectation and predictions of the inevitability of the transition from capitalism to socialism and eventually classless communist society based upon it.

Two comments are in order. Firstly, while this failure involves an astounding misreading of Marxian texts, neither book is rejected in toto; both are valuable in other respects. Secondly, the conception of the dialectic of forces and relations of production as the motive power of historical development and transformations is by no means considered valid by this writer. The point, however, is that it should be recognised as a weakness in Marx' and Engels' historical materialism, and the theoretical and strategic implications of its shortcomings dealt with, rather than evading them by failing to accept its reality. In this way, the critique is in continuation of that made of other texts in *Experience and Historical Materialism* and *Structure, Agency and Theory*, and serves as a warning to readers not to consider the latter proved wrong by Mau or Meiksins Wood.

This is not just a matter of getting the record straight, though it is also that; as noted in *A Critique of Mau: Mute Compulsion*, Mau's and Meiksins Wood's misreading of Marx reduces the failure of his (and Engels') expectations and predictions about the inevitability of the supersession of capitalism to come true to a *theoretical* non-problem *and* glosses over a yawning gap in terms of revolutionary-socialist *strategy*.

Hindess & Hirst's argument is rejected in its entirety. The critique of it is mainly made because it forms a link between Althusserian structuralism on the one hand and Laclau & Mouffe's discourse-analytical approach and Keith Jenkins' postmodernist rejection of history as a discipline on the other, and thus a continuation of the critique of discourse analysis in *Structure, Agency and Theory*, and of both in *Experience and Historical Materialism*.

The three next essays are made to counter critique of *Structure, Agency and Theory* and the argument on Marxian historical materialism in that and *Experience and Historical Materialism*, and some critique that might be made against some of the argument in the latter, more specifically in its Afterword. The first of them is a slightly modified translation of a paper read by this writer at a gathering in Copenhagen on 16 March 2022 arranged by the Institute of Marxist Analysis, setting forth some of the argument in *Structure, Agency and Theory*. The second one deals with critique against it made by a reviewer and at the said gathering. And the third one argues that some points which may seem provocative in the Afterword of *Experience and Historical Materialism* are actually at least to some extent vindicated by textual evidence. The closing seventh essay deals with the problem of reading Marx, with Mau as an example.

Readers may wonder why so much is made of Mau's and Meiksins Wood's misreadings of Marx, with so much going over the same terrain, and the same Marxian texts, twice or more. One answer is that this is part of an effort to demonstrate the very *fact* of these misreadings *and* suggest how surprising they are, or should be: how strange it is that people with such excellent qualifications for getting Marx' (and Engels') historical materialism right nevertheless get it so wrong in spite of the available evidence. Apart from methodical problems with the actual way of reading and interpreting this evidence, one cause would seem to be the hardening of a certain line of interpretation into an orthodoxy in various quarters, but no definitive explanation can be offered here.

Finally, a word on quotations. The essays have been written over a period of time, with no original plan to publish them together. As they turn, to a considerable degree, on related issues, quotations, often of considerable length, of or from the same passages tend to recur; apart from saving the trouble of inserting cross-references from essay to essay, it is probably more convenient for readers to be able to read them in the different contexts of the individual essays rather than having to leaf back to a previous one. As for the length of the quotations, the very extent to which Marx and Engels have been misinterpreted, often flagrantly inconsistently with the textual evidence, testifies to the need for careful documentation.

1. A Critique of Mau: *Mute Compulsion*.

If a somewhat "long series of quotations the aim of which is to prove that the presented reading is correct" is admissible, a critical examination of the argument on Marxian determinism in Mau's *Mute Compulsion* is relevant. Firstly, because this book, which is a serious and otherwise valuable work in many ways, is so much at variance with the argument on this subject in *Structure, Agency and Theory*. Secondly, because it is likely to be widely read by people interested in historical materialism, and may well be referred to as an authoritative text by those critical towards such arguments on Marxian determinism[1] as that in *Structure, Agency and Theory*. Thirdly, as an illustration of the extent to which the misreading of Marx and Engels to the effect that they did *not* consider the transition from capitalism to socialism and eventually classless communist society inevitable has become a kind of orthodoxy the substantiation of which is partly "done" by reference to various authorities, partly by reference to textual evidence which does not, in fact, support it. And fourthly, because Mau is indeed fundamentally wrong about a crucial aspect of Marx' (and Engels') historical materialism, their conception of the dialectic of forces and relations of production as the motive power of historical development and transformations. Readers of *Mute Compulsion* should be made aware of this, even if they may find much of interest in the book too. The mute compulsion of capitalist economic relations[2] has not, to be sure, actually been forgotten in the Marxist tradition,[3] but it is still an important point

---

[1] Determinism, that is, in the sense of considering the transition from capitalism to socialism and eventually classless communism inevitable.

[2] Marx, *Das Kapital*, 1, p. 765.

[3] Dobb, p. 7-8, p. 10, p. 16-17. Anderson, *Lineages of the Absolutist State*, p. 403-404. Sørensen, p. 172-173. Laclau, *Politics and Ideology in Marxist Theory*, p. 75. Therborn, p. 30. Cohen, p. 83. Gram-Jensen,

which is worthy of the renewed attention drawn to it by Mau, whose book contains several interesting observations.

Readers may wonder about this positive evaluation of *Mute Compulsion* as a whole on the one hand and the perhaps rather harsh criticism in this essay on the other. The explanation is, however, quite simple. In his Introduction to the book, Mau writes:

> This book is not a Marxological treatise; its ultimate aim is to understand *capitalism*, not Marx. Sometimes, however, the former presupposes the latter. For this reason, I do occasionally engage in discussions of Marx's intellectual development and other topics that might seem to be merely Marxological intricacies – but only when they ultimately help us understand capitalism.[4]

Mute Compulsion does contribute to the understanding of capitalism, especially the economic power of capitalism. Marx' intellectual development is a secondary matter in it, but one on which the argument is so faulty that a warning against accepting it is called for – and *this* is the subject of this essay.

Before entering into the main quarrel with Mau's reading of Marx, it may, as more than just a kind of curiosity, be noted that his reading of Parsons is misleading too. Parsons is given rather short shrift: "It is not uncommon to come across references to Marx in debates on power in social sciences. Some scholars are rather dismissive; Talcott Parsons, for example,

---

Structure, Agency and Theory, p. 312, p. 320-321, p. 535, and, more obliquely, p. 482, p. 498, p. 543-544, p. 546-547.
[4] Mau, p. 12.

regards Marx's critique of capitalism as outdated, empiricist political economy."[5] Actually, Parsons writes:

> The permanent importance of the Marxian exploitation theory for the present discussion lies, however, not in these peculiar technicalities which are now mainly only of antiquarian interest. It lies rather in the fact that, starting as Marx did from the element of class conflict, the center of his attention was on bargaining power. Thus in a particular case he reintroduced the factor of differences of power into social thinking, which had been so important in Hobbes' philosophy and so neglected since. The particular classical trappings of the theory are of quite secondary importance and their correction in terms of modern economic theory does not alter the essentials, though it does the form of statement and some of the secondary results.[6]

This is not quite as dismissive as one would think from Mau's words. Indeed, in a note to this paragraph Parsons warns against "throwing out the baby with the bath" by repudiating Marx altogether, adding that modern economist "have done this essentially because they have in general shared the implicit assumption of a natural identity of interests."[7] In fact the paragraph just quoted, and the following one,[8] might seem to point towards a notion of "mute coercion" inherent in capitalist relations. And at a later point, Parsons *does* deliver what is in effect a summary of that notion:

---

[5] Mau, p. 29-30. Cf. Parsons, p. 108-110. In the Danish edition, the reference is, correctly, to Parsons, *The Structure of Social Action* (New York & London: The Free Press & Collier-Macmillan, 1966), p. 108 ff, p. 489. In the English edition it is to Parsons, "Power and the Social System" in Lukes, *Power*, 108 ff, 489).

[6] Parsons, p. 109.

[7] Parsons, p. 109 (note 2).

[8] Parsons, p. 109-110.

Marx, through his doctrine of interests, elevated not only competition but the whole structure of the economic order into a great control mechanism, a compulsive system. This is the essential meaning of Marx's conception of economic determinism. It is not a matter of psychological antirationalism, but of the total consequences of a multitude of rational acts. On the one hand, the system itself is the resultant of the myriad of individual acts but, on the other, it creates for each acting individual a specific situation which compels him to act in certain ways if he is not to go contrary to his interest. Thus for Marx exploitation was to be blamed on neither the unreasonableness nor the plain selfishness of the individual employer, but the employer was placed in a situation where he must act as he did, or be eliminated in the competitive struggle.

Thus, while "liberal" theory focused its main attention on the superior efficiency of an individualistic order, Marx stressed its compulsive aspect and through this the total structure of the system. The system itself would be thought of as self-acting. Once the individuals involved in it are placed in the situations that are given, their actions are "determined" so as to maintain the system as a whole, or rather drive it forward on the evolutionary course, to end at last in its self-destruction.[9]

Parsons has been quoted at some length, partly to suggest what is meant by the mute compulsion of capitalist economic relations, although Parsons does not, in the quoted passages, spell out the specific compulsion on agents without means of production apart from their labour-power to put this labour-

---

[9] Parsons, p. 491-492.

power up for sale, thus making it possible for the owners of capital to appropriate surplus value and/or surplus labour from them. And partly to draw attention to the weakness of Mau's *reading* of this theorist, a weakness which, as will be shown below, is also demonstrable in his reading of Marx himself.

Returning, therefore, to Mau, he offers a definition of the interaction between social circumstances and agency which is unobjectionable:

> What drives history is not the immanent and necessary development of the productive forces, but human beings acting within a set of determinate social structures from which certain tendencies arise. Some modes of production thwart technological development, others – such as capitalism – accelerate some forms of it.[10]

But before that, he makes the following assertion, which must be quoted at full length:

> The primacy ascribed to productive forces in orthodox historical materialism is, as I have already mentioned, also possible to find in many of Marx's writings. In *The German Ideology*, he and Engels are quite unambiguous: 'In the development of productive forces there comes a stage when productive forces and means of intercourse are brought into being which, under the existing relations, only cause mischief, and are no longer productive but destructive forces.' In this familiar scheme, the relations of production are that variable which adapts to the immanently developing productive forces. This position is restated in writings such as *The Poverty of Philosophy* and the *Communist Manifesto* and

---

[10] Mau, p. 108.

achieved its paradigmatic formulation in the preface to the *Contribution to the Critique of Political Economy* (quoted in chapter three). As he delved into a detailed study of technology in the early 1860s, however, Marx changed his views. He now began to regard the development of the productive forces as a *result* of the relations of production. Apparently, Marx did not realise just how significant a theoretical change this was, and he continued to hold on to some of the core ideas of productive force determinism in some of his writings from the 1860s. Perhaps the best example is a famous passage from chapter thirty-two of the first volume of *Capital*, where he claims that 'capitalist production begets, with the inexorability of a natural process, its own negation'. As Heinrich has rightly pointed out, however, this passage is merely 'declamatory' and does not constitute a 'prerequisite for [the] essential arguments of the critique of political economy'. Marx's productive force determinism relies on the unwarranted assumption of a transhistorically necessary tendency for the productive forces to develop, regardless of the specific relations of production under which they are put to use – an assumption which is essentially *external* to Marx's general theoretical framework. After the publication of the French edition of the first volume of *Capital* (1872-75) – the last edition Marx prepared – productive force determinism disappears entirely from his writings. Towards the end of his life, he even explicitly opposed determinist readings of his work. In a 1877 letter to the editors of a Russian journal, Marx stressed that the sections on so-called primitive accumulation in *Capital* was no more than a 'historical sketch of the genesis of capitalism in Western Europe', not 'a historico-philosophical theory of general development, imposed by fate on all peoples, whatever the historical circumstances in which they are placed'. He restated this point in his letter to Vera Zasulich from 1881, where he underlined that his analysis of 'the "historical inevitability" of this process is *expressly* limited to the *countries of Western Europe*'.[11]

This is a mind-boggling misreading of Marx. For one thing, one should not confuse the question of *primitive accumulation in different societies* (Western and non-Western) with that of Marx' (and Engels') predictions of *the inevitable supersession of capitalism by socialism and eventually classless communist society*, one of which is made in the *Manifesto* of 1848[12] *and* quoted, along with a new one on the same page, in *Capital*.[13] For another, in his letter to the editorial board of the *Otechestvenniye Zapiski*, Marx writes that,

> The chapter on primitive accumulation does not pretend to do more than trace the path by which, in Western Europe, the capitalist order of economy emerged from the womb of the feudal order of economy. [.....]. At the end of the chapter [on primitive accumulation – I. G.-J.] the historical tendency of production is summed up thus: That it "itself begets its own negation with the inexorability which governs the metamorphoses of nature"; that it has itself created the elements of a new economic order, by giving the greatest impulse at once to the productive forces of social labour and to the integral development of every individual producer; that capitalist property, resting already, as it actually does, on a collective mode of production, cannot but transform itself into social property. At this point I have not furnished any proof, for the good

---

[11] Mau, p. 107-108.

[12] Marx & Engels, *Manifest der Kommunistischen Partei*, p. 474; cf. ibid., I, passim.

[13] Marx, *Das Kapital*, 1, p. 790-791.

reason that this statement is itself nothing but a general summary of long expositions previously given in the chapters on capitalist production.[14]

Along with the prediction of the expropriation of the expropriators, (accompanied, as in *Capital*, by the explanation, in terms of the conception of the dialectic of forces and relations of production as the motive power of historical development and transformations, why petty industry was superseded by capitalist production in the course of primitive accumulation), this assertion about the negation of the negation is quoted in *Anti-Dühring*, written 1876-1878 and published 1878, where the conception of the dialectic of forces and relations of production as the motive power of the supersession of capitalism, through the agency of the working class, is emphasised for all it is worth.[15]

The assertion that the passage is merely declamatory[16] is not supported by the textual evidence. It is, in fact, an integral part of a summary of the transition from small-scale industry

---

[14] Marx, ["Brief an die Redaktion der "Otetschestwennyje Sapiski""], p. 108-111 (translation from Marx & Engels, *Selected Correspondence*, Progress Publishers, Moscow, 1965, p. 312). Cf. Marx, *Das Kapital*, 1, p. 791 ("*Aber die kapitalistische Produktion erzeugt mit der Notwendigkeit eines Naturprozesses ihre eigene Negation.*")

[15] Engels, *Anti-Dühring*, p. 159-161 (*MEW*, 20, p. 123-124 (Marx, *Das Kapital*, 1, ch. 24.7), p. 188-189 (*MEW*, 20, p. 146-147), Part III, ch. II, passim. In his introductory note to the French edition of Engels' *Die Entwicklung des Sozialismus von der Utopie zur Wissenschaft*, written about 4/5 May 1880, Marx recommended *Anti-Dühring* as to some extent an *introduction to scientific socialism* (*MEW*, 19, p. 181-185). His and Engels' cooperation in the process of writing *Anti-Dühring* (*Anti-Dühring*, p. 13-14 (*MEW*, 20, p. 9)) is corroborated by *MEW*, 34, p. 34, p. 36, p. 37, p. 39-40.

[16] For this, Mau refers to Michael Heinrich, "Geschichtsphilosophie bei Marx" in Diethard Behrens (ed.), *Geschichtsphilosophie oder Das Begreifen der Historizität*, Freiburg, ca ira, 1999.

based on the private property of the workers in their means of production to capitalism and further to "social property", accounted for in terms of the conception of the dialectic of forces and relations of production as the motive power of historical development and transformations (and, as suggested by Marx in his letter to the editorial board, part of the overall context of the analysis of *Capital*, vol. 1). As Marx writes about the supersession of the first-mentioned mode of production by capitalism:

> This mode of production presupposes the fragmentation of holdings, and the dispersal of the other means of production. As it excludes the concentration of these means of production, so it also excludes co-operation, division labour within each separate process of production, the social control and regulation of the forces of nature, and the free development of the productive forces of society. It is compatible only with a system of production and a society moving within narrow limits which are of natural origin. To perpetuate it would be, as Pecqueur rightly says, 'to decree universal mediocrity'. At a certain stage of development, it brings into the world the material means of its own destruction. From that moment, new forces and passions which feel themselves to be fettered by that society. It has to be annihilated; it is annihilated.[17]

The precise place of the "famous passage" in the context may best be demonstrated by quoting the three last paragraphs, of which this passage is the second, of the chapter – at the

---

[17] Marx, *Das Kapital*, 1, p. 789 (translation of the following passages from Alan W. Wood, *Marx Selections*, p. 272-274). Cf. Marx & Engels, *Manifest der Kommunistischen Partei*, p. 467-474, Marx, "Marx an Pawel Wassiljewitsch Annenkow in Paris, 28. Dezember [1846]", p. 549, and Marx, *Das Elend der Philosophie*, p. 140-141.

undeniable price of a rather long quotation. Small-scale industry society had to be, and was, annihilated, and the direct producers expropriated. Eventually, with developed capitalism, "What is now to be expropriated is not the self-employed worker, but the capitalist who exploits a large number of workers."

> This expropriation is accomplished through the action of the immanent laws of capitalist production itself, through the centralization of capitals. One capitalist always strikes down many others. Hand in hand with this centralization, or this expropriation of many capitalists by a few, other developments take place on an ever-increasing scale, such as the growth of the co-operative form of the labour process, the conscious technical application of science, the planned exploitation of the soil, the transformation of the means of labour into forms in which they can only be used in common, the economizing of all means of production by their use as the means of production of combined, socialized labour, the entanglement of all peoples in the net of the world market, and, with this, the growth of the international character of the capitalist regime. Along with the constant decrease in the number of capitalist magnates, who usurp and monopolize all the advantages of this process of transformation, the mass of misery, oppression, slavery, degradation and exploitation grows; but with this there also grows the revolt of the working class, a class constantly increasing in numbers, and trained, united and organized by the very mechanism of the capitalist process of production. The centralization of the means of production and the socialization of labour reach a point at which they become incompatible with their capitalist integument. This integument is burst asunder. The knell of

capitalist private property sounds. The expropriators are expropriated.

The capitalist mode of appropriation, which springs from the capitalist mode of production, produces capitalist private property. This is the first negation of individual private property, as founded on the labour of its proprietor. But capitalist production begets, with the inexorability of a natural process, its own negation. This is the negation of the negation. It does not reestablish private property, but it does indeed establish individual property on the basis of the achievements of the capitalist era: namely co-operation and the possession in common of the land and the means of production produced by labour itself.

The transformation of scattered private property resting on the personal labour of the individuals themselves into capitalist private property is naturally an incomparably more protracted, violent and difficult process than the transformation of capitalist private property, which in fact already rests on the carrying on of production by society, into social property. In the former case, it was a matter of the expropriation of the mass of the people by a few usurpers; but in this case, we have the expropriation of a few usurpers by the mass of the people.[18]

So, Marx himself does not seem to have considered the prediction of the inevitable "negation" of capitalism "essentially *external*" to his general theoretical framework. Nor, indeed,

---

[18] Marx, *Das Kapital*, 1, p. 790-791. At the end of the last paragraph, the footnote is inserted quoting the prediction in the *Manifesto* (*MEW*, 4, p. 474) of the defeat of the bourgeoisie and the victory of the working class as inevitable.

does there seem to be any sound reason to think that it is merely declamatory. It is, to be sure, not derived from his analysis of *Capital*, but a core element of the "general conclusion" and "guiding principle of my studies" he arrived at in the course of his studies of political economy in Paris and Brussels and summarised in the "15 sentences" in the Preface to *A Contribution to the Critique of Political Economy* dated January 1859.[19] While it cannot be said to be well-founded theoretically, and is, in the opinion of this writer, actually wrong, there is no doubt that it informed Marx' strategic outlook to the end of his intellectual career.[20]

Indeed, the prediction of the inevitable supersession of capitalism is actually *repeated* in the two first of his four drafts of 1881[21] of the letter to Vera Zasulich which is cited by Mau to support his assertion that Marx "explicitly opposed determinist readings of his work":

> Another circumstance favourable to the maintenance of the Russian Commune (in its development) is that it is not merely contemporary with capitalist production and has also lived beyond the period in which this social system was still found to be intact, whereas today, no less in Western Europe than in the United States, this social system finds itself at war with

---

[19] Marx, *A Contribution to the Critique of Political Economy*, p. 20-22 (*MEW*, 13, p. 8-11). Marx was expelled from France in January 1845, and from Belgium in March 1848 (Wheen, p. 90, p. 126); as the conception of the dialectic of forces and relations of production as the motive power of historical development and transformations is traceable at least as early as *Die deutsche Ideologie*, written (*MEW*, 3, p. 10), 1845-46 (p. 72-73, p. 212, p. 338, p. 424), Marx' dating seems correct).

[20] Cf. *Structure, Agency and Theory*, Part One, ch.s 2-3 and Appendix Three.

[21] *MEW*, 19, p. 572 (note 155), p. 618

science, with the popular masses and with the forces of production it begets. In a word, it finds capitalism in a crisis which will only end with its abolition, with the return of modern societies to the "archaic" form of common property [.....].[22]

Above all, in Western Europe the ruin of common property and the rise of capitalist production are separated by a huge timespan comprising a whole series of successive economic revolutions and evolutions of which capitalist production is only the latest. On the one hand it has developed the social productive forces eminently, on the other hand it has shown its own incompatibility with the forces of its own making. Its history is nothing but a history of antagonisms, crises, conflicts and disasters. Finally, it has revealed its purely transitional nature to the whole world except those who are blind because of their interests.[23]

According to these drafts, capitalism finds itself at war "with the forces of production it begets" and "has shown its own incompatibility with the forces of its own making." The accordance of these remarks with the argument in the first section of the *Manifesto*, sentence 5-7 of the "15 sentences" in the preface to *A Contribution to the Critique of Political Economy*,[24]

---

[22] Marx, ["Entwürfe einer Antwort auf den Brief von V. I. Sassulitsch"], p. 385-386; cf. p. 390 ("in a word, it goes through a crisis which will end with the abolition of capitalism and the return of modern society to a higher form of the "archaic" type of collective possession and collective production"), p. 392, p. 397-398.
[23] Marx, ["Entwürfe einer Antwort auf den Brief von V. I. Sassulitsch"], p. 397, cf. p. 397-398.
[24] Marx, *A Contribution to the Critique of Political Economy*, p. 21 (*MEW*, 13, p. 9): "At a certain state of development, the material productive forces of society come into conflict with the existing relations of production or – this merely expresses the same thing in legal terms

Capital, 1, ch. 24.7, and *Anti-Dühring*, Part III, ch. II,[25] is unmistakable. And as these drafts, as well as *Anti-Dühring*, and Marx' letter to the editorial board of the *Otechestvenniye Zapiski*, are *later* than the publication of the French edition of the first volume of *Capital*, Mau's proposition that Marx' "productive force determinism", his expectation that the transition from capitalism to socialism and eventually classless communist society is inevitable, "seems to disappear entirely from his writings" from the latter point in time is quite simply wrong.

Marx does reject determinism in *one* context: primitive accumulation,[26] but *not* in another: the supersession of capitalism by socialism and eventually classless communist society. Unless one specifies about *what* Marx is supposed to nourish or not nourish determinist ideas, the discussion about determinism or no determinism easily becomes futile. What is argued here and in *Structure, Agency and Theory* is that Marx and Engels were determinists in the precise sense of expecting and predicting that the transition from capitalism to socialism and eventually classless communist society is inevitable. The (*as it*

– with the property relations within the framework of which they have operated hitherto. From forms of development of the productive forces these relations turn into their fetters. Then begins and era of social revolution."

[25] Just two quotations to exemplify the point: "*The contradiction between socialized production and capitalistic appropriation manifested itself as the antagonism of proletariat and bourgeoisie.*" (p. 321; *MEW*, 20, p. 253); and, "*the productive forces are in rebellion against the mode of production which they have outgrown.*" (p. 327; *MEW*, 20, p. 258).

[26] The letter actually sent to Vera Zasulich rejects nothing more than that the analysis of the primitive accumulation in *Capital* deals with more than that process in Western Europe; it does not deal with the question of the transition from capitalism to socialism and eventually classless communist society, and whether it is inevitable or not, at all (Marx, [Brief an V. I. Sassulitsch, 8. März 1881] (*MEW*, 19)/ "Marx an Vera Iwanowna Sassulitsch in Genf, 8. März 1881" (*MEW*, 35)).

is untenable) basis of their expectations and predictions is their conception of the dialectic of forces and relations of production as the motive power of historical development and transformations – classically formulated in Marx' 1859 Preface to *A Contribution to the Critique of Political Economy* (but running through their texts from at least *Die deutsche Ideologie* to Marx' first two drafts of his letter to Vera Zasulich, that is, in effect, to the end of his intellectual career) – involving the assumption that the class with an interest in the continued development of the productive forces will accomplish a historical transformation (revolution) when this development has been fettered by the relations of production.[27] Mau completely fails to read Marx correctly here. Finally, he quotes a passage from Marx' 1861-63 Manuscripts which goes:

> *Natural laws of production!* Here, it is true, it is a matter of the *natural laws of bourgeois production*, hence of the laws within which production occurs at a particular historical stage and under *particular historical conditions of production*. If there were no such laws, the *system of bourgeois production* would be altogether incomprehensible [*unbegreiflich*]. What is involved here, therefore, is the presentation of *the nature* of this particular mode of production, hence its *natural laws*. But just as it is itself *historical*, so are its *nature* and the *laws of that nature*. The natural laws of the Asiatic, the ancient, or the feudal mode of production were essentially different.

To which Mau adds the comment that, "So, the expression 'natural laws' refers to the *essential* and historically *specific* determinations of a mode of production, not to the way in

---

[27] Marx, "Marx an Pawel Wassiljewitsch Annenkow in Paris, 28. Dezember [1846]", p. 549; *Das Elend der Philosophie*, p. 140-141; *A Contribution to the Critique of Political Economy*, p. 21 (*MEW*, 13, p. 9). See, further, *Structure, Agency and Theory*, Part One, ch.s 2-3 and Appendix Three for documentation.

which a transhistorical technological drive smashes through the fetters of historical particularities.[28]

Once again, Mau makes an interpretation which Marx' words do not support. Firstly, it is of course a truism that different modes of production are qualitatively different from each other in terms of the conditions for production and their developmental "laws" or logics: otherwise, they would not be different modes. But the passage does *not* state that there are no "laws", whether one likes to call them "natural" or "social", or "(trans)historical", of historical transitions from one mode of production (and type of society) to another. And Mau seems to overlook, or ignore, that Marx had no problem with the words of a Russian reviewer that,

> For Marx only one thing is important: to find the law of the phenomena the investigation of which he is engaged in. And not only the law ruling them insofar as they have a finished form and constitute a whole [*in einem zusammenhang stehn*], as they are observed in a given period, is important to him. Most important of all to him is the law of their transformation, their development, i. e. their transition from one form to another, from one order of the whole to another. [.....] it is quite sufficient when, along with the necessity of the present order, he demonstrates at the same time the necessity of a different order into which the former must pass, quite regardless of people believing it or not, of their being conscious or unconscious of this. Marx considers the social movement a process of natural history ruled by laws that are not only independent of the will, consciousness and intentions of people, but on the contrary determine their will, consciousness and intentions. [.....] The scientific value of such

---

28 Mau, p. 108-109.

investigation lies in the explanation [*Aufklärung*] of the specific laws ruling the origin, existence, development, death of a given social organism and its substitution by another, higher one. And the book by Marx actually has this value.[29]

Marx quoted this in his "Afterword" to the second edition of *Capital*, and added this comment: "Depicting what he calls my real method so accurately [*treffend*] and, as far as my personal application of it is concerned, so favourably, what has the author depicted but the dialectical method?"[30]

When a book of such merit as Mau's *Mute Compulsion* contains such mistakes as those pointed out here, the non-determinist nature of Marx' historical materialism (perhaps a mature, or late, version of it) has certainly (but erroneously) become an established "fact", or one might say, orthodoxy.[31] This is to some extent understandable, as it reduces the failure of Marx' and Engels' expectations and predictions about the supersession of capitalism to come true to a *theoretical* non-problem, but on the other hand it glosses over a yawning gap in terms of revolutionary-socialist *strategy*. Marx' 1859 Preface posits that,

> [.....]. No social order is ever destroyed before all the productive forces for which it is sufficient have been developed, and new superior relations of production never replace older ones before the material conditions for their existence have matured within the framework of the old society. Mankind thus inevitably

[29] Marx, *Das Kapital*, 1, p. 25-27; cf. p. 15-16.
[30] Marx, *Das Kapital*, 1, p. 25-27. The "Afterword" is dated 24 January 1873.
[31] The second essay in *Experience and Historical Materialism* offers a series of examples of such readings of Marx. Cf. *Structure, Agency and Theory*, Part One, ch.s 2-3.

sets itself only such tasks as it is able to solve, since closer examination will always show that the problem itself arises only when the material conditions for its solution are already present or at least in the course of formation.[32]

This is nothing less than a promise that neither the actual transition from capitalism to socialism, nor the eventual transition from socialism to classless communism, that is, the establishment of the *effectively* collective command of the means, process and outcome of production at a sufficiently high[33] level will offer insuperable problems. Not only is the question of *class capacities* thus in effect considered non-existent,[34] the experience of post-1917 "real existing socialism" suggests that there are indeed real problems and pitfalls involved in such a process, just as the twentieth-century record of advanced capitalist societies suggest that they have more stamina than expected.

This does *not* mean that Marx' analysis and critique of capitalism as an exploitative, antagonistic, alienating and crisis-ridden and, in human terms, irrational mode of production is wrong, nor that historical materialism as an approach to the study of society and history should be abandoned. But it does suggest that the elaboration of a *realistic* strategy for the transition from capitalism to socialism and further to classless communist society in the abovementioned sense is an urgently necessary task.

---

[32] Marx, *A Contribution to the Critique of Political Economy*, p. 21 (*MEW*, 13, p. 9).

[33] And, as it must of course be added from our experience today, *sustainable* production at that level.

[34] See on this Levine & Wright and Wright, Levine & Sober, Part I.

2. A Critical Comment on Meiksins Wood: "History or Technological Determinism?"

a.

This essay deals specifically with the fourth of the nine essays in Ellen Meiksins Wood's *Democracy Against Capitalism: Renewing Historical Materialism*, "History or technological determinism?", which was not discussed in either *Structure, Agency and Theory*, or *Experience and Historical Materialism*, and which turns on precisely the questions of the conception of the dialectic of forces and relations of production as the motive power of historical development and transformations, and determinism in Marx' (and Engels') historical materialism. The critique of Meiksins Wood's argument does not, then, imply any critique of the other essays in her book, which are indeed both very interesting and brilliant. The term "determinism" is used in the same sense as in *Agency, Structure and History* and *Experience and Historical Materialism*: "the belief that some long-term terminus of human (pre-)history or the development of capitalism, such as a transition to socialism and eventually communism, can be predicted with certainty".[35]

---

[35] *Structure, Agency and Theory*, p. 1328; cf. *Experience and Historical Materialism*, p. 64 for the somewhat narrower definition as "the expectation and prediction that capitalism is bound to be superseded by socialism and eventually classless communist society" (it should, hopefully, be obvious that "classless capitalist society" which is actually written on the page is an error!). If not quite identical, the two definitions are interconnected, as both beliefs are based on the conception of the dialectic of forces and relations of production as the motive power of historical development and transformations, and their strategic implications in terms of the transition from capitalism to socialism and eventually classless communist society are identical and for obvious reasons pivotal to the discussions about that conception and the expectations and predictions based on it. There is, consequently, no reason to distinguish between them in

On p. 129, Meiksins Wood emphatically rejects the idea of the conception of the dialectic of forces and relations of production as a central element in Marx' theory of history:

> What, then of the proposition that history is propelled forward by the inevitable *contradictions* between forces and relations of production? This proposition is often regarded as the central tenet of Marx's theory of history and deserves close and critical scrutiny.
>
> The principle in question goes something like this: Forces of production tend to develop. At some point, they come up against the limits imposed by production relations which make further development impossible. This contradiction compels productive forces to break through the restrictive integument, requiring relations of production to change and allowing forces to advance. The main canonical source for this proposition is Marx's 1859 Preface to *The Critique of Political Economy*, and I have no intention of denying this textual warrant; nor do I intend to enter into a debate about the textual evidence or about its significance, except to say that both Marxists and their critics have placed an enormous theoretical burden upon Marx's short-hand aphorisms – notably those about the contradictions between forces and relations of production, and those about 'base' and 'superstructure' – without taking account of their rarity or their poetic allusiveness and economy of expression, and without putting into the balance the weight of his whole life's work and what it tells us about his theoretical principles. But with or without Marx's imprimatur, the principle of

---

the following discussion: the second simply denotes a specific case of the belief denoted by the first one.

contradiction between forces and relations of production demands exploration.

It might seem superfluous to enter into this, as various denials of determinism in Marx' and Engels' historical materialism have been sufficiently proved wrong in *Structure, Agency and Theory* and *Experience and Historical Materialism*.[36] But, firstly, a survey of the weaknesses of the conception of the dialectic of forces and relations of production as the motive power of historical development and transformations may be useful in its own right. Secondly, when such an acute historical materialist as Meiksins Wood tries to make light of "the proposition that history is propelled forward by the inevitable *contradictions* between forces and relations of production", her argument cannot be passed over in silence. And in terms of reading Marx and Engels, Meiksins Wood's argument is unsound.

In the first place, and unlike the base-and-superstructure metaphor, the conception of the dialectic of forces and relations of production as the motive power of historical development and transformations is no short-hand aphorism, and there is nothing poetic or allusive about it; it is a main element in Marx' general conclusion serving as the guiding principles of his studies ["*Das allgemeinen Resultat, das sich mir ergab und, einmal gewonnen, meinem Studien zum Leitfaden diente*"], spelled out by 5-12 and 14-15 of the 15 sentences sketching that conclusion:

> [.....]. In the social production of their existence, men inevitably enter into definite relations, which are independent of their will, namely relations of production appropriate to a given stage in the development of their material forces of production. The totality of

---

[36] *Structure, Agency and Theory*, Part One, ch.s 2-3 and Appendix Three; *Experience and Historical Materialism*, "Reading Marx".

these relations of production constitutes the economic structure of society, the real foundation, on which arises a legal and political superstructure and to which correspond definite forms of social consciousness. The mode of production of material life conditions the general process of social, political and intellectual life. It is not the consciousness of men that determines their existence, but their social existence that determines their consciousness. At a certain stage of development, the material productive forces of society come into conflict with the existing relations of production or – this merely expresses the same thing in legal terms – with the property relations within the framework of which they have operated hitherto. From forms of development of the productive forces these relations turn into their fetters. Then begins an era of social revolution. The changes in the economic foundation lead sooner or later to the transformation of the whole immense superstructure. In studying such transformations it is always necessary to distinguish between the material transformation of the economic conditions of production, which can be determined with the precision of natural science, and the legal, political, religious, artistic or philosophic – in short, ideological forms in which men become conscious of this conflict and fight it out. Just as one does not judge an individual by what he thinks about himself, so one cannot judge such a period of transformation by its consciousness, but, on the contrary, this consciousness must be explained from the contradictions of material life, from the conflict existing between the social forces of production and the relations of production. No social order is ever destroyed before all the productive forces for which it is sufficient have been developed, and new superior relations of production never replace older ones before the material conditions for their existence have matured within the framework of the old society. Mankind thus inevitably sets itself only such tasks as it is able to solve, since closer examination will always show that the problem itself arises only when the material conditions for its solution are already present or at least in the course of formation. In broad outline, the Asiatic, ancient, feudal and modern bourgeois modes of production may be designated as epochs marking progress in the economic development of society. The bourgeois mode of production is the last antagonistic form of the social process of production – antagonistic not in the sense of individual antagonism but of an antagonism that emanates from the individuals' social conditions of existence – but the productive forces developing within bourgeois society create also the material conditions for a solution of this antagonism. The prehistory of human society accordingly closes with this social formation.[37]

Meiksins Wood's summary of "the principle in question", quoted above, referring to this passage in the 1859 Preface, is, probably inadvertently, misleading: Marx does not assert that, "This contradiction compels productive forces to break through the restrictive integument, requiring relations of production to change and allowing forces to advance." In the 1859 Preface, according to Meiksins Wood "The main canonical source for this proposition", it is stated that, "men become conscious of this conflict and fight it out", and in other texts, quoted below, such as Marx' letter to Annenkow, the *Manifesto*, *Capital*, 1, ch. 24.7 and *Anti-Dühring*, it is made

---

[37] Marx, *A Contribution to the Critique of Political Economy*, p. 20-22 (*MEW*, 13, p. 8-9). Cf. Engels, *Anti-Dühring*, p. 216 (*MEW*, 20, p. 248-249 (quoted below)), a passage testifying to the continuity in Marx' and Engels' historical materialism.

perfectly clear that Marx and Engels expect the transition from one mode of production, or type of society, to another to be brought about by the class with an interest in the unfettering of the development of the productive forces.

As for the implied contrast between its "rarity" and Marx' "whole life's work", it turns up at key points throughout his and Engels' life's work, in *Die deutsche Ideologie*, *Das Elend der Philosophie*, the *Manifesto*, *Capital* and *Anti-Dühring*, to mention just those central texts.[38] In both the first section of the *Manifesto* and *Capital*, ch. 24.7, setting forth the conclusion about the historical tendency of capitalist accumulation (quoting the conclusion of the first section of the *Manifesto* in a note[39]), the conception of the dialectic of the forces and relations of production as the motive power of historical development and transformations plays a pivotal role in accounting for the transition from precapitalist to capitalist production *and* the expectation that the latter is bound to be superseded by socialism and eventually classless communist society. In *Anti-Dühring*, Part III, ch. 2,[40] it looms equally large:

> [.....]. The greater the mastery obtained by the new mode of production over all decisive fields of production and in all economically decisive countries, the

---

[38] This is shown in *Structure, Agency and Theory*, Part One, ch.s 2-3 and Appendix Three, and in the second essay in *Experience and Historical Materialism*. The passage in *Grundrisse*, p. 749-750 and that in Marx' letter to Annenkow of 28 December 1846, p. 549 (cf. the one in *Das Elend der Philosophie*, p. 140-141), may be emphasised too.

[39] Marx, *Das Kapital*, 1, p. 791 (note 252).

[40] Cf. also Engels, *Anti-Dühring*, p. 188-189 (*MEW*, 20, p. 146-147); and p. 159-160 (*MEW*, 20, p. 123-124), where Marx, *Das Kapital*, 1, p. 790-791 is quoted, after a short summary of the preceding pages on the transition from feudal production to petty-bourgeois production and on to capitalist production, in terms of the dialectic of forces and relations of production.

more it reduced individual production to an insignificant residuum, *the more clearly was brought out the incompatibility of socialized production with capitalistic appropriation.*[41]

The contradiction between socialized production and capitalistic appropriation manifested itself as the antagonism of proletariat and bourgeoisie.[42]

The contradiction between socialized production and capitalistic appropriation now presents itself as *an antagonism between the organization of production in the individual workshop and the anarchy of production in society generally.*[43]

In these crises, the contradiction between socialized production and capitalist appropriation ends in a violent explosion. The circulation of commodities is, for the time being, stopped. Money, the means of circulation, becomes a hindrance to circulation. All the laws of production and circulation of commodities are turned upside down. The economic collision has reached its apogee. *The mode of production is in rebellion against the mode of exchange, the productive forces are in rebellion against the mode of production which they have outgrown.*[44]

Whilst the capitalist mode of production more and more completely transforms the great majority of the population into proletarians, it creates the power which, under penalty of its own destruction, is forced to accomplish this revolution. Whilst it forces on more and more the transformation of the vast means of

[41] Engels, *Anti-Dühring*, p. 321 (*MEW*, 20, p. 252).
[42] Engels, *Anti-Dühring*, p. 321 (*MEW*, 20, p. 253).
[43] Engels, *Anti-Dühring*, p. 324 (*MEW*, 20, p. 255).
[44] Engels, *Anti-Dühring*, p. 327 (*MEW*, 20, p. 257-258); cf. p. 327-328 (*MEW*, 20, p. 258).

production, already socialized, into state property, it shows itself the way to accomplishing this revolution. *The proletariat seizes political power and turns the means of production in the first instance into state property.*[45]

With all the weaknesses of the conception of the dialectic of forces and relations of production, what is allusive about these passages? Or the other ones referred to above? But the misinterpretation in Meiksins Wood does not end there. A few pages further on, she suggests that,

> Still the principle of contradiction between forces and relations of production may have a more specific and fruitful meaning, if we cease to treat it as a general law of history – a law so general as to be vacuous – and regard it as a law of *capitalist* development, a principle internal to the capitalist mode of production from its inception to its decline, a statement about its specific dynamic and internal contradictions. Indeed it is precisely, and only, in this specific application that the principle received any detailed elaboration from Marx himself – and in such a way that it appears not as a general law but as a characteristic specific to capitalism, an account of those very contradictions that are associated with the uniquely capitalist drive to revolutionize productive forces.[46]

It is surely significant that in Marx's own accounts of historical transitions the development of productive forces plays little role as the primary motor. This is true even in his explanation of the transition from

---

[45] Engels, *Anti-Dühring*, p. 332 (*MEW*, 20, p. 261); cf. ff, especially p. 335-336 (*MEW*, 20, p. 264) on the leap from the realm of necessity to the realm of freedom in consequence of this revolution.
[46] Meiksins Wood, p. 135. She refers to Marx, *Das Kapital*, 3, p. 260.

feudalism to capitalism. His most comprehensive accounts of pre-capitalist societies in the *Grundrisse*, and of the historical transition to capitalism – especially in the section on 'Primitive Accumulation' in *Capital* – do not invoke the development of productive forces as the motivating impulse of historical change. They are, in fact, based on the premise that what needs to be explained is precisely the origin of capitalism's distinctive drive to improve the forces of production.[47]

There is, however, an explicit explanation of the historical transition from feudalism to capitalism in Marx' letter to Annenkow of 28 December 1846 in terms of the dialectic of forces and relations of production.

> M. Proudhon mixes up ideas and things. People [*die Menschen*] never relinquish what they have won, but this does not mean that they never relinquish the social form in which they have acquired certain productive forces. Quite the contrary. In order not to lose the results attained, in order not to forfeit the fruits of civilisation, people are obliged, as soon as their mode of carrying on commerce no longer corresponds to the productive forces acquired, to change all their inherited social forms. I am using the word "commerce" here in the widest sense it has in German: *Verkehr*. For example: the privileges, the institution of guilds and corporations, the whole regulatory regime of the Middle Ages, were social relations that solely corresponded to the acquired productive forces and to the previously existing state of society from which these institutions had arisen. Under the protection of the corporative and regulatory regime, capital was accumulated, overseas trade was developed, colonies were

---

[47] Meiksins Wood, p. 137.

founded – and people would precisely have forfeited these fruits if they had tried to retain the forms under whose shelter these fruits had ripened. Hence there were two thunderclaps, the revolution of 1640 and that of 1688. All old economic forms, the social relations corresponding to them, the political order which was the official expression of the old society, were shattered in England. Thus the economic forms in which people produce, consume and exchange are *transitory and historical*. With the acquisition of new productive forces people change their mode of production, and with the mode of production they change all economic circumstances that were merely the relations necessary for this particular mode of production.[48]

The same explanation, is, although more briefly, given in the *Manifesto*:

We see then: the means of production and of exchange, on whose foundation the bourgeoisie built itself up, were generated in feudal society. At a certain stage in the development of these means of production and of exchange, the conditions under which feudal society produced and exchanged, the feudal organization of agriculture and manufacturing industry, in one word, the feudal relations of property became no longer compatible with the already developed productive forces; they became so many fetters. They had to be burst asunder. They were burst asunder.[49]

---

[48] *MEW*, 4, p. 549; translation from *Marx Selections: Edited, with Introduction, Notes, and Bibliography, by Allen W. Wood*, p. 112 (modified to bring it closer to the German translation in *MEW*). Cf *Das Elend der Philosophie*, p. 139-141.
[49] Marx & Engels, *Manifest der Kommunistischen Partei*, p. 467.

Moreover, Marx *does*, in *Das Kapital*, 1, chapter 24.7 on the historical tendency of capitalist accumulation, explain the destruction of small-scale production by producers owning their own means of production precisely in terms of the limits on the development of the productive forces imposed by this mode of production. The relevant passages in *Capital*, 1, ch. 24.7, leading up to that on the transition from capitalism to socialism, go:

> The private property of the worker in his means of production is the foundation of small-scale industry, and small-scale industry is a necessary condition for the development of social production and the free individuality of the worker himself. Of course, this mode of production also exists under slavery, serfdom and other situations of dependence. But it flourishes, unleashes the whole of its energy, attains its adequate classical form, only where the worker is the free proprietor of the conditions of his labour, and sets them in motion himself: where the peasant owns the land he cultivates, or the artisan owns the tool with which he is an accomplished performer.

> This mode of production presupposes the fragmentation of holdings, and the dispersal of the other means of production. As it excludes the concentration of these means of production, so it also excludes co-operation, division of labour within each separate process of production, the social control and regulation of the forces of nature, and the free development of the productive forces of society. It is compatible only with a system of production and a society moving within narrow limits which are of natural origin. To perpetuate it would be, as Pecqueur rightly says, 'to decree universal mediocrity'. At a certain stage of development, it brings into the world the material means of its own

destruction. From that moment, new forces and new passions spring up in the bosom of society, forces and passions which feel themselves to be fettered by that society. It has to be annihilated; it is annihilated. Its annihilation, the transformation of the individualized and scattered means of production into socially concentrated means of production, the transformation, therefore, of the dwarf-like property of the many into the giant property of the few, and the expropriation of the great mass of the people from the soil, from the means of subsistence and from the instruments of labour, this terrible and arduously accomplished expropriation of the mass of the people forms the pre-history of capital. It comprises a whole series of forcible methods, and we have only passed in review those that have been epoch-making as methods of the primitive accumulation of capital. The expropriation of the direct producers was accomplished by means of the most merciless barbarism, and under the stimulus of the most infamous, the most sordid, the most petty and the most odious of passions. Private property which is personally earned, i.e., which is based, as it were, on the fusing together of the isolated, independent working individual with the conditions of his labour, is supplanted by capitalist private property, which rests on the exploitation of alien, but formally free labour.

As soon as this metamorphosis has sufficiently decomposed the old society throughout its depth and breath, as soon as the workers have been turned into proletarians, and their means of labour into capital, as soon as the capitalist mode of production stands on its own feet, the further socialization of labour and the further transformation of the soil and other means of production into socially exploited and therefore

42

communal means of production takes on a new form. What is now to be expropriated is not the self-employed worker, but the capitalist who exploits a large number of workers.[50]

Whatever changes in Marx' conception of the genesis of capitalism may have occurred between e. g. his letter to Annenkow or the *Manifesto* on the one hand and *Capital* on the other, what is this if not an explanation of the historical transition to capitalism in terms of the dialectic of forces and relations of production? There is no basis for making a fundamental distinction in this respect between the early Marx on the one hand and the mature Marx and *Capital* on the other.[51]

b.

Marx' main emphasis is certainly on the dialectic of forces and relations of production as the motive power of the transformation from capitalism and to socialism and eventually classless communist society. But this is, after all, to be expected inasmuch as capitalist, not feudal, society or petty production was – and is – the exploitative type of society to be overcome.

---

[50] Marx, *Das Kapital*, 1, p. 789-790 (Translation (by Ben Fowkes) in Alan W. Wood (ed.), *Marx Selections*, p. 272-273 (Marx, *Capital*, Volume 1, Pelican Marx Library, Random House, New York 1974)).

[51] As Meiksins Wood, following Brenner, does. According to Meiksins Wood, Brenner "distinguishes between two kinds of historical theories in Marx's own work, the first still heavily reliant on the mechanical materialism and economic determinism of the eighteenth-century Enlightenment, the second emerging out of Marx's mature critique of classical political economy." (p. 115. Cf. p. 120 for the assertion that Brenner questions "the historical-materialist credentials of such a theory by attributing it to an undeveloped phase of Marx's work, still uncritically bound to classical bourgeois thought").

Moreover, the issue is not whether the conception of the dialectic of forces and relations of production as the motive power of historical development and transformations is valid for precapitalist history or not: this writer agrees that it is not. If anything, the issue is whether it makes sense when applied to *capitalist* development. And here again, the most plausible answer is that it does not. In the first place, it seems to offer no guarantees about future capitalist development or the supersession of capitalism *unless* the revolutionary consequences of the fettering of the development of the productive forces by the relations of production is demonstrated to be a law of *previous* historical transformations.

And the conception of the dialectic of forces and relations of production as the motive power of historical development and transformation suffers from several other, and serious, weaknesses.

In the first place, it seems doubtful if the development of the productive forces is actually *fettered* by capitalist relations of production in the sense in which that expression is used in Marx' letter to Annenkow, the *Manifesto*, the 1859 "Preface", *Capital* and *Anti-Dühring*. In a speech made in 1856, Marx predicted the abolition of capitalism at the hands of the proletariat, but while he gave a very persuasive description of the paradox that although the development of the productive forces in its capitalist framework creates the potential for the satisfaction of multiple human needs, and many-sided human creativity and development, capitalism exerts a pressure towards mass poverty and the stunting of human and social development, this does not mean that the capitalist social order is not sufficient enough for the further development of the productive forces:

> The so-called revolutions of 1848 were but wretched episodes – small fractures and fissures in the hard crust

of European society. Nevertheless, they revealed an abyss. Beneath the apparently solid surface they betrayed oceans of liquid matter, only needing expansion to rend into fragments continents of hard rock. Noisily and confusedly, they proclaimed the emancipation of the proletarian, i. e. the secret of the nineteenth century, and of the revolution of that century.

That social revolution was, to be sure, no novelty invented in 1848. Steam, electricity, and the self-acting mule were revolutionists of a much more dangerous character than even citizens Barbès, Raspail and Blanqui. But, although the atmosphere in which we live weighs upon every one with a 20,000 lb. force, do you feel it? No more than European society before 1848 felt the revolutionary atmosphere enveloping and pressing it from all sides.

There is one great fact, characteristic of this our nineteenth century, a fact which no party dares to deny. On the one hand, industrial and scientific forces have been aroused which no epoch of former human history ever suspected. On the other hand, there are symptoms of decay far surpassing the horrors told of the latter times of the Roman Empire.

In our days everything seems pregnant with its opposite. We see that machinery, endowed with the wonderful power of shortening human labour and making it more fruitful, stuns it and sucks it dry to the point of exhaustion. By some strange magic curse, the new sources of wealth are turned into sources of want. The victories of science seem bought with a loss of character. To the same extent as mankind masters nature, man seems conquered by other men or his own baseness. Even the pure light of science only seems able to shine against the dark background of ignorance. All our inventiveness and our whole progress seem to end up endowing material forces with intellectual life and reducing human life to a dull material force. This antagonism between modern industry and science on the one hand and modern misery and decay on the other, this antagonism between the forces of production and the social relations of our epoch is a palpable, overwhelming and undeniable fact. In certain quarters this may be lamented; others may wish to rid themselves of modern technical achievements in order to rid themselves of modern conflicts. Or they may imagine that such remarkable progress in industry requires an equally remarkable regress in politics to be complete. As for ourselves, we do not fail to recognise the shape of the cunning spirit persistently manifesting itself in all these contradictions. We know that to take real effect the new forces of society only need new men to become their masters – and these are the workers.

They are as much an invention of the new age as the machinery itself. In the signs that puzzle the bourgeoisie, the nobility and the miserable prophets of reaction, we recognise our brave friend Robin Goodfellow, the old mole capable of such swift undermining, that excellent sapper – the revolution. The English workers are the first-born sons of modern industry. Hence, they will certainly not be the last to aid the revolution bred by this industry, a revolution which means the emancipation of their own class in the whole world, which is as universal as the sway of capital and wage slavery. I know the heroic struggles the English working class has gone through since the middle of the previous century – struggles that are only little known because they are shrouded in darkness and the bourgeois historians suppress them.

In the Middle Ages there was a secret tribunal called the *Femgericht*. It was there to take revenge for the misdeeds of the ruling class. When you found a house marked with a red cross, then you knew that the owner had been convicted by the *Fem*. Today all houses in Europe are marked with the mysterious red cross. History is the judge – the proletarian its executioner.[52]

In his letter to Annenkow, Marx argues that actors effect the transition from precapitalist to capitalist relations in order not to be deprived of the results which have been attained by the development of productive forces within the framework of the former, which have now become fetters on the further development of the forces of production. In his 1856 speech, he predicts that the proletariat will do away with the effects of capitalist *development* of the productive forces, to realise the potential for human and social development this development creates while at the same time preventing its realisation. The conflict between forces and relations of production is not quite identical in the two cases, although a class with an interest in the supersession of the dominant relations of production is identifiable in both. But in any case, the question of *class capacities* (for struggle) – "the organizational, ideological and material resources available to class agents"[53] – cannot be ignored: the ability of the class with an interest in a historical transformation to organise around this interest and realise it cannot be *taken for granted* except on *teleological-*

---

[52] Marx, "Rede auf der Jahresfeier des "People's Paper" am 14. April 1856 in London". Cf. Meiksins Wood, p. 119-121 on "the specific imperative of capitalism to improve the forces of production". It is of course true, as both she and Marx observe (p. 125), that the capitalist pressure for the development of the productive forces has nothing to do with any aim of lightening workers' toil.
[53] Levine & Wright, passim. Wright, Levine & Sober, Part I (definition quoted from p. 29).

functionalist assumptions, which Marx and Engels explicitly rejected in *Die heilige Familie* and *Die deutsche Ideologie*.[54] In *Structure, Agency and Theory*, Part Four, ch. 1. d, it is demonstrated that Cohen's attempt to overcome these problems is unsuccessful.[55] That is, *either* we have to give up the assumption that an era of (successful) social revolution begins when the relations of production turn into fetters on the development of the productive forces, *or* we have to assume that historical development is ruled by a teleological-functionalist logic allowing us to assume that, "No social order is ever destroyed before all the productive forces for which it is sufficient have been developed," and that, "Mankind thus inevitably sets itself only such tasks as it is able to solve, since closer examination will always show that the problem itself arises only when the material conditions for its solution are already present or at least in the process of formation."[56]

The textual evidence contradicting Meiksins Wood's conclusion quoted above from p. 129 is, in fact, irrefutable. But how does she arrive at that position? By emphasising the *unique* pressure for the development of the productive forces in capitalism, in contradistinction to precapitalist modes. Having quoted a critic of historical materialism who argues that, "Explaining the singularity of capitalist development generates a most fundamental criticism of the Marxian scheme of historical interpretation", she comments that,

> John Gray is here so precisely on the mark in his insistence on the singularity of capitalism and his

---

[54] Marx & Engels, *Die heilige Familie*, p. 98; *Die deutsche Ideologie*, p. 46. Cf. Engels, *Anti-Dühring*, p. 84, p. 89 (*MEW*, 20, p. 61-62, p. 66-67).

[55] Cohen, *Karl Marx's Theory of History: A Defence*, ch.s IX-X.

[56] That "new superior relations of production never replace older ones before the material conditions for their existence have matured within the framework of the old society" is obviously an unobjectionable assumption – indeed a truism.

characterization of that system as uniquely driven by a 'powerful incentive' to revolutionize productive forces, that it seems churlish to point out that Marx thought of it first. Indeed, this insight into the specificity of capitalism is the essence of Marx's critique of political economy.[57]

And further:

A stress on the uniqueness of capitalism and its developmental drive – and the denial of unilinearism that this implies – is therefore not an aberration or a momentary, if fatal, lapse in Marxism. It is deeply embedded in and intrinsic to Marx's own analysis from the start. This alone should put us on guard against any easy assumption that the 'abandonment' of a unilinear determinism strikes at the heart of the Marxist project.[58]

Where, then, do the forces of production figure in all this? The proposition that history is simply the inexorable progress of productive forces is vacuous and by itself inconsistent with Marx's analysis of capitalism.[59]

Again, the centrality of the conception of the dialectic of forces and relations of production as the motive power of historical development and transformations in Marx' and Engels' mature work is too well-documented for Meiksins Wood's conclusion to be acceptable. How, then, is an awareness of the uniqueness of capitalism to be fitted into the picture?

---

[57] Meiksins Wood, p. 123-124. Cf. ff., and p. 119-120, p.
[58] Meiksins Wood, p. 125-126.
[59] Meiksins Wood, p. 127-128.

Marx was *certainly* aware of the *unique* pressure of capitalism for the development of the productive forces, as against precapitalist modes/types of society. But this, it would seem from the evidence, had precisely the effect that he (and Engels) made what one might call a projection backwards into precapitalist history: capitalism replaced precapitalist relations of production *because* the latter had become fetters on the development of the productive forces; and those precapitalist relations had replaced earlier ones *because* those earlier ones had become fetters on the development of the productive forces – and now, *capitalist* relations were turning into fetters on that development, and *because of that*, and through the agency of the capitalist working class, capitalism would now be replaced by socialism and eventually classless communist society. This is spelled out in the *Manifesto*, in *Capital*, 1, ch. 24.7 and in *Anti-Dühring*. The great impetus given to the development of the productive forces by the transition to capitalism is, it seems, in effect generalised into the conception of the dialectic of forces and relations of production as the motive power of historical development and transformations – in stark contradistinction to Meiksins Wood's argument that it demonstrates the absence (or marginality?) of that conception in Marx' mature work.

It is, then, at least a reasonable hypothesis that the industrial revolution within a capitalist framework, with its accelerated development of the productive forces, is actually at the root of the conception of the dialectic of forces and relations of production as the motive power of historical development and transformations: reasonable because it is consistent with the textual evidence. But on the other hand, this conception cannot be considered to be based on a longer historical perspective or the analysis in depth of earlier historical transformations. It is thus hardly unfair to hypothesise that Marx and Engels offered a general explanation of historical transformation on an inadequate basis: the pressure for development of the productive forces exercised by the capitalist mode and the contrast between capitalist and precapitalist societies in this regard. The weakness of this explanation is also suggested by the distance between their predictions and the actual historical development since the start of the 20th century – not least as far as working-class consciousness and politics are concerned.[60]

The fundamental weakness of the conception of the dialectic of forces and relations of production as the motive power of historical development and transformations is, then, that it is, in effect, dependent on the teleological-functionalist assumption that historical development and transformations are ruled by an *intentional* logic. We can only speak rationally about *intentions* and *objectives* of *agents/actors* – that is, if not necessarily human actors, then at least creatures with some degree of consciousness, not e. g. structures, modes of production or history.

The conclusion is, then, that the conception of the dialectic of forces and relations of production as the motive power of historical development and transformations should be abandoned in favour of that of history as the interaction between social circumstances and agency. This also means that Marx' and Engels' confidence in the transition from capitalism to

---

[60] One may also note two loose ends in the work of Marx and Engels in this context: firstly, the eventuality of the common ruin of the contending classes mentioned in the *Manifesto* (*MEW*, 4, p. 420), referring to the possibility of a society being conquered by foreigners introducing novel relations of production (cf. Marx & Engels, *Die deutsche Ideologie*, p. 23-24, for examples. Cf. Meiksins Wood, p. 131). And secondly, the concept of *the Asiatic mode of production* in which there is no real development of the forces of production (Marx, *Das Kapital*, 1, p. 377-379) – so that there is, in effect, no dialectic of forces and relations of production, and no internal motive power of social development and transformations.

socialism and eventually classless communist society as inevitable has to be abandoned; such a transition cannot be ruled out, but it cannot be taken for granted that it is bound to happen. And this suggests the most problematic aspect of the conception of the dialectic of forces and relations of production as the motive power of historical development and transformations and its weaknesses: the fact that the abandonment of Marx' and Engels' expectations and predictions, and the consequent notion of history as open-ended, *leave us with a strategic gap*: where Marx and Engels were confident that the transition from capitalism to socialism and eventually classless communist society is both possible and inevitable according to the assurance given in the 1859 "Preface", we must to accept that we have to *find out* how to accomplish it, without any certainty that it *will* prove possible to do so.

What is the nature – and problem – of the said gap left by the weaknesses of the conception of the dialectic of forces and relations of production as the motive power of historical development and transformations? It would seem to be twofold. Firstly, as just noted we cannot be *certain* that the class capacities of the working class are – or can be made – sufficient for the task of accomplishing the transition to socialism and further to classless communist society – whether, that is, it can be sufficiently organised around its fundamental class interest in this transition *and* develop, and realise, the right strategy for accomplishing it. And secondly, we cannot be *certain* whether or not the *effectively* collective command of the means, process and outcome of production can actually be established *and* function as a system of production at a sufficiently high – *and* sustainable – level.

Given the nature and effects of capitalism known not just from Marxist analysis, but certainly no less from historical experience, this lack of guarantees that a revolutionary-socialist agenda is realisable should not lead to the conclusion that the attempt to realise it should be abandoned. But it does involve an immense task of organisation and of analysis and theoretical development and debates, not just in academia, but in, and on the development of, working-class organisations. And one fundamental quality of it must be the uncompromisingly *democratic* nature of this work in all its aspects, as an absolutely necessary condition of its success: no effectively collective command of the means, process and outcome of production can be developed by means of undemocratic organisations, discussions and decision-making. This consistent adherence to democracy will no doubt imply its own problems in terms of adaptability and tactical agility in the face of adversity, resistance and especially downright oppression, but it is essential to avoid impeding or even stifling the development of theory and practice, and to prevent the emergence of new class divisions. The realm of freedom cannot be based on the centralisation of effective power.

To return to Meiksins Wood, her critique (p. 127-134) of "the principle of contradiction between forces and relations of production" (p. 134) as an explanation of historical development and transformation is cogent, but the same is not true of the presentation of it as, at the most, marginal to Marx' and Engels' own historical materialism. It *is* their fundamental explanation of historical development and transformations, albeit in a kind of uneasy tandem with their conception of agents as the makers of their own history in the given circumstances at any given point in time. The following passage demonstrates her way of explaining away this obvious reading of their relevant texts:

> This principle of contradiction can, with caution, be used to illuminate retrospectively the transition from feudalism to capitalism. It suggests that a mode of production whose internal principle of motion was to revolutionize productive forces could not have come

about without a transformation in the relations of production and class. But the meaning of such retrospective formulations, in which historical *consequences* are described as if they were causes, should not be misconstrued. This is one of Marx's favourite ploys – as in the famous proposition that 'Human anatomy contains a key to the anatomy of the ape'; and it is often mistaken for teleology. In this case, Marx's formulation simply means that the drive to transform productive forces was not the cause but the result of a transformation in the relations of production and class.[61]

Meiksins Wood's assertion that Marx (and Engels) did not consider the contradiction between forces and relations of production, the drive to transform productive forces, the cause of the transition from precapitalist to capitalist relations of production is flatly contradicted by the paragraph in the *Manifesto* which has already been quoted above:

> We see then: the means of production and of exchange, on whose foundations the bourgeoisie built itself up, were generated in feudal society. At a certain stage in the development of these means of production and of exchange, the conditions under which feudal society produced and exchanged, the feudal organization of agriculture and manufacturing industry, in one word, the feudal relations of property became no longer compatible with the already developed productive forces; they became so many fetters. They had to be burst asunder; they were burst asunder.[62]

---

[61] Meiksins Wood, p. 136; cf. p. 139-140.
[62] Marx & Engels, *Manifest der Kommunistischen Partei*, p. 467. Cf. Marx, "Marx and Pawel Wassiljewitsch Annenkow in Paris, 28. Dezember [1846]", p. 549, *Das Elend der Philosophie*, p. 140-141, and *Das Kapital*, 1, p. 789-790 (and Engels, *Anti-Dühring*, p. 159 (*MEW*, 20, p. 123), where the argument in *Das Kapital*, 1 is repeated).

Meiksins Wood asserts that, "It is especially ironic that the strategy adopted by Marx to highlight the specificity of capitalism has been mistaken for a teleological account of history".[63] But the point is not that Marx and Engels argued that historical development is a teleological process: they explicitly and repeatedly denied that it is. The point is that their conception of the dialectic of forces and relations of production as the motive power of historical development, and their confidence that capitalism will be superseded by socialism and eventually classless communist society which is derived from it, lack cogency *except* on teleological assumptions.

c.

The consequent tension in their historical materialism is clearly visible when one compares Marx' words in *The Eighteenth Brumaire of Louis Bonaparte* on human agents as the makers of their own history, although always under the given and inherited circumstances with which they are directly confronted, and with the tradition of the dead generations weighing like a nightmare on the minds of the living,[64] or those quoted above from his letter to Annenkow of 28 December 1846, with the following ones in the review he approvingly quotes in the Afterword to the second edition of the first volume of *Capital*:

> For Marx only one thing is important: to find the law of the phenomena the investigation of which he is engaged in. And not only the law ruling them insofar as they have a finished form and constitute a whole [*in einem zusammenhang stehn*], as they are observed in a given period, is important to him. Most important of

---

[63] Meiksins Wood, p. 139.
[64] Marx, *The Eighteenth Brumaire of Louis Bonaparte*, p. 146 (*MEW*, 8, p. 115).

55

all to him is the law of their transformation, their development, i. e. their transition from one form to another, from one order of the whole to another. [.....] it is quite sufficient when, along with the necessity of the present order, he demonstrates at the same time the necessity of a different order into which the former must pass, quite regardless of people believing it or not, of their being conscious or unconscious of this. Marx considers the social movement a process of natural history ruled by laws that are not only independent of the will, consciousness and intentions of people, but on the contrary determine their will, consciousness and intentions. [.....] The scientific value of such investigation lies in the explanation [*Aufklärung*] of the specific laws ruling the origin, existence, development, death of a given social organism and its substitution by another, higher one. And the book by Marx actually has this value.[65]

What the words in *The Eighteenth Brumaire* and in the letter to Annenkow, or for that matter those in the *Manifesto*, do not explain is what guarantee there is that the will, consciousness and intentions, and the other necessary class capacities, of the class with an interest in the continued development of the productive forces will indeed be present when it is fettered by the relations of production – in other words, what ensures that this fettering will indeed usher in an era of social revolution, in which "mankind", or more precisely the said class, will prove itself capable of accomplishing the historical transformation providing the solution to the problem of that fettering. And in effect the reviewer only, or so at least it would seem, spells out the logic of Marx' remark that,

---

[65] Marx, *Das Kapital*, 1, p. 25-27; cf. p. 15-16.

[.....]. Even when a society has got on the scent of the natural law of its motion – and the ultimate purpose of this work is to disclose the economic law of motion [*das ökonomische Bewegungsgesetz*] of modern society – it can neither skip natural phases of development [*naturgemäße Entwicklungsphasen*] nor abolish them by decree. But it can shorten and alleviate the birth-pangs.[66]

The logical answer to the question is that the natural law of motion of society is that given by the reviewer, namely that the natural law of motion of (capitalist) society, or the laws ruling the natural process of the social movement, also determine(s) the will, consciousness and intentions of people, with the result that the historical transformation required to unfetter the development of the productive forces is accomplished. The problem with this conception is that it implies, against Marx' and Engels' own words in *Die heilige Familie* and *Die deutsche Ideologie*, a notion of *teleological*, and hence *closed*, history using human agents for its own ends. On the other hand, this conception seems to be the only alternative to that of an *open-ended* process of historical development, with no guarantees that the transition from capitalism to socialism and eventually classless communist society *will* indeed be accomplished.

It should, however, be noted that perhaps Marx, rightly or wrongly, read, and endorsed, the reviewers' words about laws determining the will, consciousness and intentions of people in the sense that when the development of the productive forces are fettered by the relations of production, agents in the class with an interest in the continued development of the productive forces will realise this interest and pursue this end. If so, his endorsement is consistent with the passage in his

---

[66] Marx, *Das Kapital*, 1, p. 15-16; cf. p. 12.

letter to Annenkow quoted above, and with the rejection of teleological conceptions of historical development in *Die heilige Familie* and *Die deutsche Ideologie*.[67] We cannot know for sure, but a reading avoiding the assumption of glaring inconsistencies in Marx and Engels is, other things equal, preferable. But *if* Marx (and perhaps also the reviewer) should be read in this sense, we are back with the question of class capacities and the *open-ended* process of historical development implied by the interaction between social circumstances and agency – in other words, with the lack of *guarantees* that the supersession of capitalism by socialism and eventually communism will take place.[68] So, the tension in Marx' and Engels' historical materialism is not eliminated: *either* agency is reducible to the mere support of an effectively teleological dialectic of forces and relations of production, *or* Marx' and Engels' expectations and predictions that this supersession is inevitable are unfounded.

It is very likely that the notion of "natural laws of motion" of societies and capitalist production came naturally to Marx and Engels because they came naturally to all students of society. As Carr observed,

> [.....]. Throughout the eighteenth and nineteenth centuries, scientists assumed that laws of nature – Newton's laws of motion, the law of gravitation, Boyle's law, the law of evolution, and so forth – had been discovered and definitely established, and that the business of the scientist was to discover and establish more

---

[67] Marx & Engels, *Die heilige Familie*, p. 98; *Die deutsche Ideologie*, p. 45.
[68] The assumption that the capitalist proletariat/working class is, or will be, *forced* to adopt and realise the objective of a transition to socialism and eventually communism by its social circumstances is, apart from the letter to Annenkow and *Anti-Dühring*, from which it is quoted above (and below), found in both *Die heilige Familie* (p. 38) and *Die deutsche Ideologie* (p. 35-36, p. 76, p. 424).

such laws by process of induction from observed facts. The word 'law' came down trailing clouds of glory from Galilei and Newton. Students of society, consciously or unconsciously desiring to assert the scientific status of their studies, adopted the same language and believed themselves to be following the same procedure. The political economists seem to have been the first in the field with Gresham's law, and Adam Smith's laws of the market. Burke appealed to 'the laws of commerce, which are the laws of nature, and consequently the Laws of God'. Malthus propounded a law of population; Lasalle an iron law of wages; and Marx in the preface to *Capital* claimed to have discovered 'the economic law of motion of modern society.[69]

This is confirmed by the following passage in the preface to *Capital*:

The physicist observes processes of nature either where they appear in their clearest form and least clouded by disturbing influences, or, where possible, he makes experiments in conditions which ensure the regular course of the process. What I have to investigate in this work is the capitalist mode of production and the corresponding relations of production and exchange. So far, their *locus classicus* is England. This is the reason why it serves as the main illustration of my theoretical exposition. However, if the German reader should pharisaically shrug off the conditions of the English industrial and agrarian labourers, or optimistically reassure himself that in Germany things are far from that bad, then I have to shout to him: De te fabula narratur!

---

[69] Carr, p. 57-58.

In itself the higher or lower stage of development of the social antagonisms that originate in the natural laws of capitalist production is not the point. The point is these laws as such, these tendencies operating and asserting themselves with inexorable necessity. The more highly industrially developed country only shows the less developed ones the picture of their own future.[70]

The question is, however, the scope of these laws of motion, that is, how much, if any, scope they leave for agency to make a difference, and whether or not they actually make it possible to predict the inevitable transition from capitalism to socialism and eventually classless communist society. For one thing, Marx' *historical* analysis in e. g. *The Eighteenth Brumaire of Louis Bonaparte* seems to give considerable emphasis to agency; and having defined "the absolute, general law of capitalist accumulation", he adds that, "Like all other laws it is modified in its eventuation by manifold circumstances the analysis of which does not belong here."[71] And yet his prediction in *Capital*, ch. 24.7 is quite unambiguous and unconditional:

> [.....]. That which is now to be expropriated is no longer the labourer working for himself, but the capitalist exploiting many labourers. This expropriation is accomplished by the action of the immanent laws of capitalistic production itself, by the concentration of capital. One capitalist always kills many. Hand in hand with this concentration, or this expropriation of many capitalists by few, develop, on an ever extending scale,

---

[70] Marx, *Das Kapital*, 1, p. 12.
[71] Marx, *Das Kapital*, 1, p. 673-674; Cf. *Das Kapital*, 3, p. 839. According to Witt-Hansen (p. 115) "absolute" is in the Hegelian sense: "abstract".

the co-operative form of the labour-process, the conscious technical application of science, the methodical cultivation of the soil, the transformation of the instruments of labour into instruments of labour only usable in common, the economizing of all means of production by their use as the means of production of combined, socialized labour. Along with the constantly diminishing number of the magnates of capital, who usurp and monopolize all advantages of this process of transformation, grows the mass of misery, oppression, slavery, degradation, exploitation; but with this too grows the revolt of the working class, a class always increasing in numbers, and disciplined, united, organized by the very mechanism of the process of capitalist production itself. Capital becomes a fetter upon the mode of production, which has sprung up and flourished along with, and under it. Concentration of the means of production and socialization of labour at last reach a point where they become incompatible with their capitalist integument. This integument is burst asunder. The knell of capitalist private property sounds. The expropriators are expropriated.[72]

But some might ask, if chapter 24.7 is about the historical *tendency* of capitalist accumulation, should we not, after all, read Marx' prediction in the same sense as his words about

---

[72] Marx, *Das Kapital*, 1, p. 790-791 (the translation is taken from Engels, *Anti-Dühring*, p. 159-160; minor textual discrepancies between various editions (see Engels, ibid., p. 160, note) are irrelevant to the present argument). Cf. *Theorien über den Mehrwert*, p. 309; *Grundrisse*, p. 331, p. 415-416, p. 460-461, p. 543, p. 749-750. Quite rightly, Allen W. Wood cites the passage as evidence that, "Marx is confident that the mass of the people will inevitably do what it has powerful, urgent, and continuing reasons to do: expropriate the expropriators and overthrow the capitalist mode of production." (*Marx Selections*, p. 16).

"the absolute, general law of capitalist accumulation", namely that "it is modified in its eventuation by manifold circumstances the analysis of which does not belong here"? So that Blackledge is right to maintain that, "At its heart, historical materialism is a theory of historical change through the evolving contradictions between the forces and relations of production of various modes of production", *and* that,

> [.....]. The possibility for a better world grew within capitalism, but this was only a possibility; and despite some ambiguous formulations to the contrary, the general thrust of both Marx's and Engel's work was a critique of political and historical fatalism. As Hobsbawm has argued Marxist historical analysis stemmed, always, from a 'commitment to politics'.[73]

This reading, to the effect that the historical tendency of capitalist accumulation only brings about the *possibility* of a transition to socialism and eventually classless communist society, would eliminate the tension between Marx' and Engels' predictions on the one hand and the open-endedness implied by the recognition of human agents as the makers of their own history on the other. But it does not stand up to closer examination. There is, firstly, to the best knowledge of this writer, no explicit utterance from either Marx or Engels supporting it, that is, to the effect that the expropriation of the expropriators should only be considered as a possibility. Marx predicts it in the straightforward future tense: "*Die Expropriateurs werden expropriiert.*" Secondly, he states in the next paragraph that, "capitalist production begets, with the inexorability of a law of nature, its own negation. It is the negation of the negation".[74] Thirdly, there is Marx' own comment on

---

[73] Blackledge, p. 146.
[74] Marx, *Das Kapital*, 1, p. 791.

Capital, 1, ch. 24.7 in his letter of November 1877 to the editorial board of the *Otechestvenniye Zapiski*:

> [.....]. At the end of the chapter the historical tendency of production is summed up thus: That it "itself begets its own negation with the inexorability which governs the metamorphoses of nature"; that it has itself created the elements of a new economic order, by giving the greatest impulse at once to the productive forces of social labour and to the integral development of every individual producer; that capitalist property, resting already, as it actually does, on a collective mode of production, cannot but transform itself into social property. At this point I have not furnished any proof, for the good reason that this statement is itself nothing but a general summary of long expositions previously given in the chapters on capitalist production.[75]

Fourthly, there is the quotation from the *Manifesto* in note 252 on the same page as Marx' prediction, including the statement that the downfall of the bourgeoisie and the victory of the proletariat are equally inevitable.[76] Fifthly, there is Engels' exposition in *Anti-Dühring*:

> [.....]. Marx merely shows from history, and here states in a summarized form, that just as formerly petty industry by its very development necessarily created the conditions of its own annihilation, i.e., of the expropriation of the small proprietors, so now the capitalist

---

[75] *MEW*, 19, p. 108-111 (translation from Marx & Engels, *Selected Correspondence*, Progress Publishers, Moscow, p. 312). The letter, which was written in French in or about November 1977, was actually never sent to the editorial board of the journal (*MEW*, 19, p. 112, p. 558 (note 69)).

[76] Marx, *Das Kapital*, 1, p. 791.

mode of production has likewise itself created the material conditions from which it must perish.[77]

And sixthly, there is Engels' account, also in *Anti-Dühring*, of the reasons for socialism's confidence in victory, an account leaving no doubt whatsoever that he (and Marx) considered the overthrow of capitalism inevitable, not a mere possibility:

> If for the impending overthrow of the present mode of distribution of the products of labour, with its crying contrasts of want and luxury, starvation and surfeit, we had no better guarantee than the consciousness that this mode of distribution is unjust, and that justice must eventually triumph, we should be in a pretty bad way, and we might have a long time to wait. The mystics of the Middle Ages who dreamed of the coming millennium were already conscious of the injustice of class antagonisms. On the threshold of modern history, three hundred and fifty years ago, Thomas Münzer proclaimed it to the world. In the English and the French bourgeois revolutions the same call resounded – and died away. And if today the same call for the abolition of class antagonisms and class distinctions, which up to 1830 had left the working and suffering classes cold, if today this call is re-echoed a millionfold, if it takes hold of one country after another in the same order and in the same degree of intensity that modern industry develops in each country, if in one generation it has gained a strength that enables it to defy all the forces combined against it and to be confident of victory in the near future – what is the reason for this? The reason is that modern large-scale industry has called into being on the one hand a proletariat, a class which for the first time in history can demand the

---

[77] Engels, *Anti-Dühring*, p. 160 (*MEW*, 20, p. 124).

abolition, not of this or that particular class organization, or of this or that particular class privilege, but of classes themselves, and which is in such a position that it must carry through this demand on pain of sinking to the level of the Chinese coolie. On the other hand this same large-scale industry has brought into being, in the bourgeoisie, a class which has the monopoly of all the instruments of production and means of subsistence, but which in each speculative boom period and in each crash that follows it proves that it has become incapable of any longer controlling the productive forces, which have grown beyond its power; a class under whose leadership society is racing to ruin like a locomotive whose jammed safety-valve the driver is too weak to open. In other words, the reason is that both the productive forces created by the modern capitalist mode of production and the system of distribution of goods established by it have come into crying contradiction with that mode of production itself, and in fact to such a degree that, if the whole of modern society is not to perish, a revolution in the mode of production and distribution must take place, a revolution which will put an end to all class distinctions. On this tangible, material fact, which is impressing itself in a more or less clear form, but with insuperable necessity, on the minds of the exploited proletarians – on this fact, and not on the conceptions of justice and injustice held by any armchair philosopher, is modern socialism's confidence in victory founded.[78]

---

[78] Engels, *Anti-Dühring*, p. 188-189 (*MEW*, 20, p. 146-147). The German text has, "*bei Strafe des Versinkens in chinesisches Kulitum*", that is, "under penalty of descending into Chinese cooliedom", which perhaps has less connotation of *purely economic* immiseration than the quoted translation.

Thus, one may conclude that the tension in Marx' and Engels' historical materialism – in the final instance a tension between the conception of the interaction between social circumstances and agency as the motive power of historical development and transformations on the one hand and that of the dialectic of forces and relations of production as that motive power on the other – *is real* and between two polar opposites: the former implying an open-ended process of historical development without any guarantee that the transition from capitalism to socialism and further to communism is inevitable; the latter a closed process of historical development the natural laws of motion of which do guarantee that transformation. Which – apart from its teleological implications – involves the problem that it does not seem to be corroborated by the historical record since the start of the twentieth century.

It is, admittedly, a strange tension, but however it is to be explained (in terms of the sources of Marx' and Engels' thinking and/or their very commitment to the class struggle against capitalism), the textual evidence demonstrating its presence in their theoretical work is unmistakable.

To make a digression here, it is hard to say what one is to make of Marx' and Engels' claims that in *The Origin of Species*, Darwin had not only given the deathblow to "teleology" in natural science, but also, according to Marx, elucidated its rational sense empirically *and*, according to Marx, delivered the natural-scientific basis of historical class struggle,[79] indeed "the basis in natural history of our view."[80] Does this reflect

---

[79] Engels, "Engels an Marx in London, 11. oder 12. Dezember 1859". Marx, "Marx and Ferdinand Lasalle in Berlin, 16. Januar 1861", p. 578.

[80] Marx, "Marx an Engels in Manchester, 19. Dezember 1860", p. 131. Marx read *The Origin of Species* in (November-)December 1860 (ibid.).

a notion of (the development of) the productive forces "selecting", by means of the class with an interest in their continued development, the relations of production more fit for them? Or what? It is hard to see the justification of the claim, precisely because Darwin's theory is explicitly non-teleological:

> [.....] natural selection, or the survival of the fittest, does not necessarily include progressive development – it only takes advantage of such variations as arise and are beneficial to each creature under its complex relations of life. And it may be asked what advantage, as far as we can see, it would be to an infusorian animalcule – to an intestinal worm, – or even to an earthworm, to be highly organised. If it were no advantage, these forms would be left, by natural selection, unimproved or little improved, and might remain for indefinite ages in their present lowly condition.[81]

As shown above, Marx and Engels claim that in capitalist crises, the productive forces *"are in rebellion against the mode of production which they have outgrown."*[82] And the chapter in which this is asserted opens with the following passage, which echoes the 1859 Preface to *A Contribution to the Critique of Political Economy*:

> The materialist conception of history starts from the proposition that the production [.....] and, next to production, the exchange of things produced, is the basis of all social structure; that in every society that has appeared in history, the manner in wealth is distributed and society divided into classes or orders is dependent upon what is produced, how it is produced, and how

---

[81] Darwin, p. 118.
[82] Engels, *Anti-Dühring*, p. 327 (*MEW*, 20, p. 258).

the products are exchanged. From this point of view the final causes of all social changes and political revolutions are to be sought, not in men's brains, not in man's better insight into eternal truth and justice, but in changes in the modes of production and exchange. They are to be sought, not in the *philosophy*, but in the *economics* of each particular epoch. The growing perception that existing social institutions are unreasonable and unjust, that reason has become unreason, and right wrong, is only proof that in the modes of production and exchange changes have silently taken place with which the social order, adapted to earlier economic conditions, is no longer in keeping. From this it also follows that the means of getting rid of the incongruities that have been brought to light must also be present, in a more or less developed condition, within the changed modes of production [*Produktionsverhältnissen*] themselves. These means are not to be *invented*, spun out of the head, but *discovered* with the aid of the head in the existing material facts of production.[83]

The last two periods of the passage are problematic: *is* the exhaustion of the progress which a given mode of production and type of society represents (or is supposed to represent) relative to the one it has superseded necessarily possible to overcome by the transition to superior relations and means of production? Could stagnation or regression also be possible? And what about class capacities?

The idea of regression to less advanced forms of life due to changed conditions of existence is perfectly compatible with Darwin's theory. But the assumption at the core of Marx' and Engels' conception of the dialectic of forces and relations of

---

[83] Engels, *Anti-Dühring*, p. 316 (*MEW*, 20, 248-249).

production as the motive power of historical development and transformations, and of their expectations and predictions, is that historical transformations caused by this dialectic are *progressive*: that is, effecting the unfettering of the development of the forces of production: implying a *closed* course of development where the implication of Darwin's argument is an *open-ended* one.

It is hard not to suspect that Marx and Engels read Darwin according to their own view, assumptions or hypothesis.[84] And one may add that tested against the history of the last, say, 150 years, their assumptions about the motive power of historical development and transformations, and their expectations and predictions of the course of history, have, alas, not been confirmed.

d.

To conclude, the presence of the conception of the dialectic of forces and relations of production as the motive power of historical development and transformations, with teleological implications, in Marx' and Engels' texts from the mid-1840s and on, including their major mature works, cannot be explained away. The fact that Marx was aware of the specificity of capitalism in terms of accelerating the development of the productive forces does not mean that we can consider that presence null and void. If anything, that specificity may have led him and Engels into the very error of assuming that a dialectic of forces and relations of production is the motive power of historical development and transformations. This explanation is, to be sure, only a hypothetical one, but it is

---

[84] The more so as Marx' 1859 Preface to *A Contribution to the Critique of Political Economy*, dated January 1859 (p. 23 (*MEW*, 13, p. 11)), preceded the publication of *The Origin of Species* (24 November 1859 (Darwin, p. 15)) by some ten months – not to mention the earlier texts by Marx and Engels in which the conception is found in more or less detail, and at more or less finished stages of development).

not unreasonable. Even if it is wrong, Meiksins Wood's conclusion is no more justified for that reason. It is correct to say that Marx and Engels do not offer any adequate justifications of their conception of the dialectic of forces and relations of production as the motive power of historical development and transformations. But the evidence that they nevertheless nourished it cannot be overlooked or refuted.

There are, then, two different theories of history[85] in Marx' and Engels' works, one of which is basically correct and productive, the other not:

1. Human agents relate *consciously* to, and act *consciously* on, their social circumstances ("lived" reality). They make their own history in the given circumstances.[86]
2. The conception of the dialectic of forces and relations of production as the motive power of historical development and transformations.

---

[85] Rigby, p. 148. *Both* theories of history are present in Marx' and Engels work at least from *Die deutsche Ideologie* and on (as documented in *Agency, Structure and Agency*), the second one very explicitly supporting their argument on the inevitable supersession of capitalism in both *Capital* and *Anti-Dühring*. In fact, the conception of the dialectic of forces and relations as the motive power of historical development and transformations is expressed in Marx' two first drafts of his reply to Vera Zasulich (*MEW*, 19, p. 385-386, p. 397), written in 1881, about two years before his death, and about 14 years after he finished the first volume of *Capital*. As far as it is concerned, Brenner's and Meiksins Wood's theoretical and chronological distinction (Meiksins Wood, p. 115 ff, p. 120) is inapplicable.

[86] Cf. Marx, *Early Writings*, p. 327-328 (*MEW, Ergänzungsband, erster Teil*, p. 515-516). Marx & Engels, *Die heilige Familie*, p. 98; *Die deutsche Ideologie*, p. 45). Marx, *The Eighteenth Brumaire of Louis Bonaparte*, p. 146 (*MEW*, 8, p. 115).

The two theories are connected, or interweaved, by the assumption that the historical transformations to which the dialectic gives rise are accomplished by the class with an interest in the continued development of the productive forces (e. g. the potential of capitalism which is released by the transcendence of precapitalist relations of production; the potential of communism to be released by the transcendence of capitalist relations of production, the leap into the realm of freedom amounting to the end of the prehistory of human society).

The first theory implies an open-ended process of historical development, especially if the importance of agents' articulation of their experiences of, and responses to, their "lived" reality[87] is recognised. The second theory implies a closed process of historical development (up to the end of the prehistory of human society). If it is abandoned, the first one, with *the conception of the interaction between social circumstances and agency as the motive power of history* remains relevant and productive, indeed indispensable if we are to acquire an adequate grasp of the process of historical development and transformations. On this point, there would seem to be no quarrel between this writer and Meiksins Wood. But her interpretation of Marx' (and Engels') historical materialism and its development is untenable.

While the first theory seems to enable us to make sense of the historical record (insofar as this can be developed from the available evidence),[88] the second theory does not, and

---

[87] As was emphasised by Thompson.
[88] This should of course not be taken to mean that a general reference to the interaction between social circumstances and agency as the cause of whatever happens will do. Quite the contrary: ideally, an exhaustive account of the process requires, firstly, a plausible demonstration that *these* experiences and responses were prompted by *those* social circumstances; and, secondly, that *this* precise interaction of these responses with each other and social circumstances

consequently it seems necessary to abandon it. And thus, the expectations and predictions about the inevitable victory of the proletariat, the inevitable transition from capitalism to socialism and eventually classless communist society, must be abandoned too.

This does not mean that the idea of a transition to socialism and eventually classless communist society defined by the collective command of the means, process and outcome of production has to be abandoned as well, as an impossible, utopian dream. But it does mean that there is no *guarantee* that it can, and indeed *will*, be accomplished. And that a realistic strategy for it – including for the organisation of a solid majority around it – must be developed rather than relying on the assurance in the 1859 Preface that the very articulation of the task proves that mankind is able to solve it. Meiksins Wood's remarks on this point are to the point:

> [.....]. If what we are dealing with is not *teleology* but *history*, then the relevant category in characterising the socialist project is not inevitability, not inescapability, not 'entelechy', not *promise*, but precisely *possibility*. And is this such an inconsiderable thing? It is not 'merely contingent, humiliatingly accidental and extraneous possibility' but *historical* possibility, that is, the existence of determinate social and material conditions which make something *possible* that was *im*possible before, conditions in which socialism can indeed be a political project and not simply an abstract ideal or a vague aspiration.

---

eventuated in *this* precise outcome. As often as not, it will probably, and perhaps most often in the first-mentioned part of the analysis, only be possible to identify the causal links with various degrees of credibility rather than certainty (and in any case with the proviso that a more cogent account may conceivably be offered in the future).

We are not obliged to accept a Manichean choice between determinism and contingency. The real alternative to both is *history*. Even a complete repudiation of 'grand narratives' in the 'post-modern' manner does not dispose of historical causality. And even at a time when history seems to be defying socialist aspirations in the most dramatic and decisive way, we need not – should not – choose between the promise of historical inevitability and the denial of any historical foundation to the socialist project.[89]

Finally, it may be observed that while the suggested conception of historical development is certainly a *revised* historical materialism, it is arguable that it remains within the Marxist tradition, inasmuch as it does not reject any of the following three assumptions the abandonment of any of which would be inconsistent with the Marxist tradition in any meaningful sense of that term:

1. Social circumstances, including such as are due to agents' positions in relations of production, are determinants of agents' consciousness.[90]
2. Capitalism is an exploitative, antagonistic, crisis-ridden and alienating mode of production.
3. The working class constituted by capitalist relations of production consequently has an objective interest in a transition from capitalism to socialism and eventually communism in the sense of a classless society based on the collective command of the means, process and outcome of production.

---

[89] Meiksins Wood, p. 144, p. 145.
[90] Determinant, that is, in the sense of delimiting a field of the possible, with pressures and probabilities.

And again, to prevent misunderstandings about this: *nothing* argued above implies that the leap into the realm of freedom Marx and Engels predicted, by means of the transition from capitalism to socialism and eventually classless communist society, is not desirable. *It is absolutely and extremely desirable.* The questions remaining to be solved are whether it will prove to be *possible*, and *how* to organise the *effectively* collective command of the means, process and outcome of production on which this classless society must be based – at a sufficiently high level of sustainable production, and with all the democratic freedoms and institutions it presupposes.

However apt Meiksins Wood's words are, they do no more than scratching the surface of the huge problematic facing any revolutionary movement, and Marxist historical materialism in particular. This is the strategic gap left by the conception of the forces and relations of production as the motive power of historical development and transformations with its promise that the problems of the transition from capitalism to socialism and classless communist society will be solvable: from the organisation of a solid majority around that fundamental working-class interest to the organisation of production and distribution within the framework of the effectively collective command of the means, process and outcome of production at a level both sustainable and high enough to prevent that scarcity provokes struggle over necessities so that "all the old shit" returns;[91] and, not to forget, sufficiently high to make an effective *defence* of the postcapitalist order against violent resistance (and economic sabotage) from within and/or without possible. These problems cannot be dealt with here, but their reality and crucial importance should be obvious enough from the historical record.

---

[91] Marx & Engels, *Die deutsche Ideologie*, p. 34-35.

3. Comments on Hindess & Hirst: *Pre-capitalist Modes of Production*.

a.

Hindess & Hirst's *Pre-Capitalist Modes of Production* contradicts Marx on at least two substantial points. Firstly, a mode of production is defined as "an articulated combination of relations and forces of production structured by the dominance of the relations of production."[92] In the Preface to *A Contribution to the Critique of Political Economy*, Marx states that, "In the social production of their existence, men [*die Menschen*] inevitably enter into definite relations, which are independent of their will, namely relations of production appropriate to a given stage in the development of their material forces of production."[93] According to this, the stage of development of the productive forces is "dominant" or determining in the combination of forces and relations of production. Secondly, Hindess & Hirst state that,

> [.....]. Central to the concept of mode of production are the concepts of *reproduction* and *limit*. Entailed in the concept of reproduction is the persistence of the structure if its conditions of existence are secured – the concept of any mode of production must define the structure of that mode as one which makes a particular form possible. The concept of *limit* specifies that the structure of a mode of production can only exist as a definite hierarchy of determinations, and that it exists as a totality only in so far as its structure in dominance and the form of action of that structure is preserved. Nothing in its concept prohibits the continued reproduction of a mode of production and nothing in its

---

[92] Hindess & Hirst, p. 9.
[93] Marx, *A Contribution to the Critique of Political Economy*, p. 20 (*MEW*, 13, p. 8).

concept requires that a mode of production transgress its own limits, i.e. dissolve itself. It is because the concept of mode of production entails the concepts of reproduction and limit that the theory of transition is a theory limited to explaining the concrete conjunctures of a transition between the dominance of one mode of production in a social formation and the dominance of another.[94]

In *Structure, Agency and Theory* and *Experience and Historical Materialism*, it has been documented that the conception of the dialectic of forces and relations of production as the motive power of historical development and transformations is found throughout Marx' and Engels' work from the mid-1840s and on.[95] There is no need to repeat that documentation here; the classical formulation of the conception is found in the 1859 Preface:

> [.....]. At a certain stage of development, the material productive forces of society come into conflict with the existing relations of production or – this merely expresses the same thing in legal terms – with the property relations within the framework of which they have operated hitherto. From forms of development of the productive forces these relations turn into their fetters. Then begins an era of social revolution. [.....] No social order is ever destroyed before all the productive forces for which it is sufficient have been developed, and new superior relations of production never replace older ones before the material conditions for their existence have matured within the framework of the old society. Mankind thus inevitably

---

[94] Hindess & Hirst, p. 202.
[95] Gram-Jensen, *Structure, Agency and Theory*, Part 1, ch.s 2-3, and Appendix Three; *Experience and Historical Materialism*, second essay.

sets itself only such tasks as it is able to solve, since closer examination will always show that the problem arises only when the material conditions for its solution are already present or at least in the course of formation. In broad outline, the Asiatic, ancient, feudal and modern bourgeois modes of production may be designated as epochs marking progress of production in the economic development of society. The bourgeois mode of production is the last antagonistic form of the social process of production – antagonistic not in the sense of individual antagonism but of an antagonism that emanates from the individuals' social conditions of existence – but the productive forces developing within bourgeois society create also the material conditions for a solution of this antagonism. The prehistory of human society accordingly closes with this social formation.[96]

This conception of the dialectic of forces and relations of production as the motive power of historical development and transformations is certainly unsound, and Hindess & Hirst's rejection of it is, to be sure, guarded in terms of their interpretation of Marx, but all the same the following must be said to give a wrong impression of his views on this point, as expressed, among other texts, in *Capital*:

> [.....]. Marxism has a non-teleological theory of history; a theory in which history has no necessity other than that produced in the conjunctures of its actual and non-pre-given course. History is not a unity with an essential structure, it has no 'end' and in it there are no 'privileged' regions or peoples. Marx undoubtedly

---

[96] Marx, *A Contribution to the Critique of Political Economy*, p. 21-22 (*MEW*, 13, p. 9). The passage confirms the dominance of (the development of) the productive forces.

remained under the influence of Hegelian ideology, particularly in respect of the East and 'Asiatic' society. The text of *Capital* contains important Hegelian elements. However, the effect of Marx's theoretical work was to produce a decisive critique of Hegel and of all teleology, and a non-Hegelian and anti-teleological theory of history. It is this theoretical work which makes possible the scientific criticism, by means of Marxist concepts, of the ideological elements in the given texts of Marx.[97]

Reading *Capital*, chapter 24.7 on "The historical Tendency of Capitalist Accumulation", especially against the backdrop of his and Engels' other central texts, it is hard not to feel that it takes a rather radical, and one-sided, belabouring of Marx to make him fit the above passage: to criticise elements in Marx by means of concepts also found in his theoretical work is one thing. To reduce that work, and "Marxism" in general, to the purged and revised edition resulting from that "scientific criticism" is another.

That point being made, the concept of a mode of production may be examined a little more closely. *In Structure, Agency and Theory*, a mode of production is described as being defined by specific relations of production, which are in their turn defined as "the combination of relations to the means of production and each other into which agents enter in their social existence, and by which a specific pattern of disposal of the means of production and the social product is established."[98]

A major difference between this concept of a mode of production and that in Hindess & Hirst is that the latter posits a

---

[97] Hindess & Hirst, p. 203-204.
[98] Gram-Jensen, *Structure, Agency and Theory*, p. 1331, p. 1333-1334.

1:1 relationship between relations and forces of production. The latter term

[.....] refers to the mode of appropriation of nature, that is, to the labour process in which a determinate raw material is transformed into a determinate product. 'The elementary factors of the labour-process are 1. The personal activity of man, i.e., work itself, 2, the subject of that work, and 3, its instruments' (*Capital*, I, p. 178). Forces of production differ according to the manner in which these elements are combined into concrete forms of the production process: the forms of co-operation and co-ordination of the labour of several individuals, the forms of articulation of the means and the object of labour with the activity of the labourers, and so on.[99]

Now the concept of a mode of production as an articulated combination of relations and forces of production precludes the construction of the concept of particular modes of production by means of the simple juxtaposition of a set of relations and a set of forces. On the contrary the concept of a particular mode of production is the concept of a determinate articulated combination of relations and forces of production. This means that there can be no definition of the relations or of the forces of production independently of the mode of production in which they are combined. [.....] Where, on the contrary, no set of corresponding productive forces can be deduced from a proposed mode of appropriation of surplus-labour, the latter belongs to no mode of production and cannot define a set of relations of production. We show in the chapter on the supposed 'Asiatic' mode of production that the

---

[99] Hindess & Hirst, p. 10-11.

concept of the appropriation of surplus-labour by the mechanism of tax/rent cannot define a set of relations of production since it belongs to no possible concept of an articulated combination of relations and forces of production.[100]

It only remains to note the level of abstraction at which this elaboration of concepts of modes of production takes place:

> The field of application of these concepts is not history. We reject the notion of history as a coherent and worthwhile object of study. These concepts are abstract, their value is not limited by the analysis of the concrete. As concepts they can have a theoretical function even if concrete conditions to which they are pertinent do not exist, have not existed and will not exist. Concepts which are not used in the analysis of concrete conditions are not therefore speculative and empty. It is empiricism which conceives the necessary field of application of all concepts as the real. In fact concepts have a valid field of application within theory.[101]

Speculative and empty or not, what happens in reality, whether in the past, the present or the future, may be considered more important than what does not exist, has not existed and will not exist. As for the concept of the 'Asiatic' mode of production, its disqualification due to the fact that, "This mode of appropriation of the surplus-product [tax/rent levied on productive units by a state which is the sole proprietor of land – I. G.-J.] corresponds to at least two distinct sets of

---

[100] Hindess & Hirst, p. 11-12.
[101] Hindess & Hirst, p. 321.

forces of production: the forces entailed in independent peasant cultivation and communal cultivation."[102] And:

> The problem of the tax/rent couple is not only that two quite distinct sets of forces of production can be derived from it but more important than this is the fact that neither of these sets of forces of production necessarily supposes relations of production which correspond to the tax/rent couple. Independent peasant production can be brought under it only on the condition of the absence of private property in land; this form of production does not presuppose this absence as a condition of its existence but it is compatible with it. Where this condition does not apply peasant production corresponds to quite different relations of production, those of the ancient mode, the 'Teutonic' mode, etc. Moreover, state property in land in the case of the tax/rent couple is a legal title imposed on the direct producers by state power – the existence of the state is its sole *raison d'être*. Communal production does presuppose the absence of private property in land, but it does not presuppose state property in land. In the case of communal production the mode of appropriation of the surplus-product and the distribution of the means of production can be by means of the institution of the collective itself.[103]

The point here is not the *label* "Asiatic mode of production", or whether or not this mode of appropriation has ever been a reality anywhere, but that it could have been a reality. It is easy to make the thought experiment of imagining a state which, having conquered a territory with independent peasant cultivation or communal cultivation, or both, declares

---

[102] Hindess & Hirst, p. 196.
[103] Hindess & Hirst, p. 196-197.

itself sole proprietor of land and levies a tax on all productive units under penalty of exclusion from land to cultivate. If so, this would, on the theoretical conditions laid down by Hindess & Hirst, be a society in which a definite mode of appropriation of the surplus-product was a reality, but which was not dominated by any mode of production, because this mode of appropriation was – or just could be, for that matter – applied to both independent and communal producers.

So maybe the real weakness is not in the notion or concept of the "Asiatic" mode of production, but in the demand that a specific set of forces of production must be deducible from a specific mode of appropriation of surplus-product. Feudal appropriation of surplus-product, it may be added, would seem equally compatible with both independent peasant cultivation and communal cultivation. Hence, one may agree with Rigby that,

> Here, however, we do not accept Hindess and Hirst's definition of a mode of production or their consequent rejection of the concept of the Asiatic mode. We can agree that a mode of production is characterised by specific relations of production, since it is precisely the variations in the forms of property which is the basis for any classification of modes of production. But there is no reason why a mode of production should be characterised by the existence of specific productive forces. The Asiatic mode is thus quite compatible with independent or communal forms of cultivation, just as primitive communism is compatible with agricultural or pre-agricultural forms of the productive forces and just as capitalism may be found in either industrial or pre-industrial forms. A mode of production is best defined as the combination of a specific set of relations of production with a potentially variable set of productive forces. The variable forms

of the labour process in the Asiatic mode allow us to define sub-forms of this mode of production rather than providing, as Hindess and Hirst claim, a refutation of the validity of this concept.[104]

b.

The suggested concept/definition of relations of production, "the combination of relations to the means of production and each other into which agents enter in their social existence, and by which a specific pattern of disposal of the means of production and the social product is established"[105] leaves room for various combinations of a. agents' relations to each other and b. their relations to their means of production, in this combination constituting modes of the appropriation of surplus labour/product/value (i. e., relations of exploitation). This does not rule out that various forms of productive forces may exclude various relations of exploitation, or render them more or less improbable; but it does not presuppose a 1:1 relationship between relations and forces of production, let alone imply any demand that the form of the productive forces can be *derived from* the relations of production if a valid *concept* of a mode of production is to be developed from the mode of appropriation.

It is definitely possible that some specific form of agents' relations to each other and their means of production may be combined with different forms of (organisation of) the process of producing the material reproduction/basis of society, e. g. by individual and collective cultivation of the land, as in Hindess & Hirst's example with the "Asiatic" mode of production.[106] In fact such flexibility must be considered an

---

[104] Rigby, p. 223-224.
[105] Gram-Jensen, *Structure, Agency and Theory*, p. 1331, p. 1333-1334.
[106] Hindess & Hirst, ch. 4.3.

augmentation of the *viability* of relations of production, and hence a mode of production, other things being equal.

An important point is precisely that combinations of agents' relations to their means of production and each other which are actually found in (past or present) history *or* are found to be *conceivable* are not disqualified because the form(s) of productive forces combined with them cannot be *derived* from them, or, more specifically, that *no single specific form* of productive forces can be derived from them.

How *different* modes of production should be distinguished from *variations* of modes of production is, logically speaking, probably best decided in terms of the likeness or differences in the precise mechanism of exploitation, emphasising the divisions between agents in terms of their relations to each other rather than the differences in terms of the productive forces and the organisation of the actual processes of production. So that for example the exploitation by *seigneurs* of individual and/or collective cultivators of the land by means of the tax/rent couple amounts to variations within a feudal mode of production/type of society (insofar as the actual process or mechanism of exploitation is modified by the difference between individual and collective cultivation), not a boundary between two different modes/types of society. This may be a field for further exploration.

That the definition of the boundary between variations in and divisions between modes of production/types of society must necessarily be a matter of analytical expediency may seem a sign of theoretical vagueness to some. Actually, however, any such retrospective breakdown of past reality will in the nature of things depend on our problematic as well as, to some extent, the available evidence. It is, again, a matter of *dialogue* between our concerns and conceptions on the one hand and the evidence of the past, with its testimony of changes and continuities, on the other: boundaries between modes of production/types of society, or between periods, are not given to us as transparent facts immediately readable from the evidence; nor are they concepts imposing themselves on us as transparently valid, relevant and necessary independently of our concerns or the evidence.

What circumstances and developments are *important?* Different people will give different answers, whether asked about the past or the present. Such judgments must be considered part, or consequence, of their articulation of their experiences of and responses to their "lived" reality. An objective criterion could be the extent and nature of the *consequences* of some circumstances and developments, although the *importance* of such consequences is, again, also to some extent dependent on various points of view; on the other hand, the causal efficacy of something (relative to that of others) is to some extent estimable, if not downright measurable.

In the present context, important areas of investigation are the origin, nature, development and solution or supersession of class antagonisms and class conflicts, the nature of the classes confronting each other or (potentially) intervening into the conflicts of other classes, the developmental logic of various modes of production and types of society, the conditions of and potential outcomes of their transcendence. And the criteria for distinguishing between different modes of production and types of society on the one hand and variants within them on the other may be defined accordingly – especially insofar as variations in different aspects tend to be interrelated. Consequently, a Marxist or historical-materialist approach will suggest defining modes of production by specific relations of production, that is, specific combinations of relations to the means of production and each other into which agents enter in their social existence, and by which a specific pattern of disposal of the means of production and the social product is established, so that the basic pattern of exploitation and consequently the class division inherent in an exploitative mode of production are determined by the relations of production; and defining types of society by the mode of production that is dominant in the respective social formations.[107] The assumption is that the dominant relations of production and the developmental logic and conditions of reproduction of the dominant mode delimit a field of the possible with pressures and different degrees of probability within which the interaction between social circumstances and agency takes place and various outcomes and social circumstances and forms eventuate and vary. Thompson has discussed this in a manner which seems more meaningful than Hindess & Hirst's demand that the forces of production can be derived from the relations of production:

> We can suppose an epochal context – feudal, capitalist, socialist – within each of which an endless variety of forms of State power, modifications of social relations, etc., may be possible. We can never guess at their range and diversity because, rich as history is, it can never exhaust possibility. But while the number of variants may be infinite, nevertheless it is infinite only within the categories of social "species." Just as, while there may be any number of permutations of breeds of dogs, and of mongrel cross-breeds, all dogs are doggy (they smell, bark, fawn on humans), so all capitalisms remain capitalist (foster acquisitive values, must by their nature leech the proletariat, etc.). The transmutation from one species to another is what we mean by revolution.[108]

---

[107] Cf. Gram-Jensen, *Structure, Agency and Theory*, p. 1331, p. 1333-1334, p. 1335.
[108] Thompson, *The Poverty of Theory and Other Essays*, p. 291-292.

In other words, as long as a specific mode defined by specific relations of production remains dominant, the development of the social formation in question belongs to the corresponding type of society, and its development can only vary within limits determined by the dominant mode, even if it may exhibit a distinctive combination of modes of production, and unique variations in terms of social struggles and economic, political and ideological forms and developments. But as Rigby observed, this limitation does not in itself imply that the productive forces can, or must be, derived from the mode of appropriation of surplus labour/surplus value.

The reference to primitive communism and capitalism points to the arbitrariness of Hindess & Hirst's rejection of the concept of the Asiatic mode of production. If primitive communism based on hunting and gathering on the one hand and primitive communism based on agriculture and animal husbandry on the other are two variants of the same mode of production, and the same goes for agricultural and industrial capitalism (with capitalism as a mode hitherto unique in its drive for development of the productive forces), why cannot the same be the case with individual and communal cultivation as the basis for the Asiatic mode of production?

It should be added that while *means of production* may be defined as the raw materials, tools, machines and propellants of any kind used in production,[109] *forces of production* should be understood to include the means of production along with *technology/know-how*, the ways in which production is *organised*, *labour-power* and of course means and organisation of *transport* insofar as it is part of the process of production.

---

[109] Including the muscular power of human beings and animals serving as a source of energy for production (e. g. in a treadmill or hoist).

The answer to the question, what is the best way to define or conceptualise a mode of production? will obviously depend on the wider theoretical context and problematic. Thus, it will make a difference whether one's point of departure is a more or less "structuralist Marxist" or Althusserian one (and despite their critique of Althusser and Balibar, Hindess & Hirst's inspiration from them is unmistakable) or the conception of the interaction between social circumstances and agency as the motive power of historical development and transformations. The demand that the forces of production can be derived from the mode of appropriation makes sense with the former, but not with the latter.

There seems to be a weird inconsistency in Hindess & Hirst's argument between their insistence that, "It is the central role of theory in Marxist politics which makes the substance of theoretical differences so important",[110] their rejection of the study of history as "not only scientifically but also politically valueless"[111] and their preoccupation with pre-capitalist modes of production, making use of historical material. Why is this exercise in pre-capitalist history, and the elaboration of concepts of pre-capitalist modes of production, relevant? Hindess & Hirst define "what we consider to be the theoretical value of the concepts presented here"[112] as follows:

> We have argued that there can be no *general* theory of modes of production. There are, however, general concepts which serve as a means of formation and of proof of concepts of specific modes of production. The concepts of the specific modes of production outlined here are not the elements of a history. They do not function as the concepts of a science of history or

---

[110] Hindess & Hirst, p. 323.
[111] Hindess & Hirst, p. 312.
[112] Hindess & Hirst, p. 322.

as the means of constitution of history as a thought object. These concepts are not about the *past* and they do not pertain to stages in a teleological process. The idea that the concepts of pre-capitalist modes, the ancient or the slave modes, for example, relate to the past is an effect of the teleological histories which have dominated Marxist theory. The conception of pre-capitalist modes of production used here does not require that, as part of their concept, such modes exist prior to capitalism or that they are necessarily succeeded by capitalism.

[.....]

The field of application of these concepts is not history. We reject the notion of history as a coherent and worthwhile object of study. These concepts are abstract, their value is not limited by the analysis of the concrete. As concepts they can have a theoretical function even if concrete conditions to which they are pertinent do not exist, have not existed and will not exist. Concepts which are not used in the analysis of concrete conditions are not therefore speculative and empty. It is empiricism which conceives the necessary field of application of all concepts as the real. In fact concepts have a valid field of application *within theory*.

The value of the concepts elaborated here is, indeed, predominantly *within theory*. There are certain concrete situations in which the concepts of the FMP [feudal mode of production – I. G.-J.], of primitive communism, and the proof that there is no valid concept of AMP [Asiatic mode of production – I. G. J.] may be useful. For example, the proof that there is no concept of AMP may have value in demonstrating the illusions and the absurd political consequences which would follow from the attempt to use such a concept to analyse the social formations of contemporary Asia. This is a secondary matter. The primary value of the concepts elaborated here is in the rectification, elaboration and development of the concept of mode of production, and in clarifying the procedures by which the concepts of specific modes of production may be formed and proved. In particular we hope that this work will be of value in contributing to the formation of an anti-historicist theory of modes of production, a theory which avoids the pitfalls of Balibar's general theory. The urgent tasks of such a theory are the development of a concept of a capitalism dominated by finance capital, a concept which builds on and goes beyond Marx's concept of the CMP [capitalist mode of production – I. G.-J.] in which industrial capital is dominant, and the development of a rigorous concept of the socialist mode of production. If this work is of service in clarifying the way to these tasks then it will have justified itself.[113]

The last period but one reveals that the concept of the capitalist mode of production does not live up to their demand that the forces of production can be derived from the mode of appropriation any more than does the concept of the Asiatic mode of production,[114] *and* that Hindess & Hirst depend on historical knowledge about the actual development of capitalism when pointing to the task of developing a concept of capitalism dominated by finance capital.

The problem with their approach and their argument is not just that they are themselves inevitably dealing with the past, arguing on the basis of historical material and interpretations.

---

[113] Hindess & Hirst, p. 320-322.
[114] Cf. Rigby, p. 223-224.

It is also that they ignore the fact that Marx and Engels did the same, and had to do so in order to grasp the nature of historical development and the capitalist mode of production.[115]

Nor is the problem with their rejection of the Asiatic mode of production just that it is based on an arbitrary demand on the conceptions of modes of production. It is also that they exclude testing their concepts of modes against past or present reality. If the tax/rent couple is found as a mode appropriation of the surplus-product corresponding to its concept in actual social formations, no amount of abstract theoretical conceptualisation can alter that fact; no introduction of conceptual constraints can prove the futility of taking it into account when analysing "the current situation" in those formations.

What precisely is this "current situation" the analysis of which, according to Hindess & Hirst, all Marxist theory exists to make possible? To present Hindess & Hirst's conception of it, yet another long passage in their own words must be quoted:

> Having defined what we consider to be the theoretical value of the concepts presented here we will attempt to specify what it is that it is the object of Marxist theory to analyse, the 'current situation'. All Marxist

---

[115] *Historical materialism* is not a label which is used by mere chance, or mistakenly. The words on Marx and Engels should not, it must be added, be read in the sense that there are no problems with their conception of the nature of historical development – their conception of the dialectic between forces and relations of production as the motive power of historical development and transformations, which is found in their texts along with that of the interaction between social circumstances and agency as that motive power, is untenable.

theory, however abstract and general, exists to make possible the analysis of the current situation. This situation must not be conceived as an object given in the real, social reality at a given moment in time. The analysis of the current situation is not a state description of the social formation. The current situation does not exist independently of the political practice which constitutes it as an object. The current situation exists for Marxist theory only in so far as it is given a definite form by Marxist political practice, and in so far as definite problems are designated as objects of analysis or criticism within the practice. These problems are problems of political practice and are specified in political terms. *What* the 'current situation' is cannot be specified in the same way that the object of an empiricist knowledge is specified. The current situation is not a definite substance, a specific unitary element of being. The analysis of the current situation is not a relation between knowledge and being, between entities. One has only to consider the situations 'current' in the works of Lenin, the objects of Lenin's analyses in different conjunctures, to see that the current situation is not one thing. These current situations do not form a unity. They do not have a single essence, a common mode of being which unifies them. The situation 'current' is now the relations between factions in the RSDLP, now the relation of the political lines of the parties in the Duma to the autocracy, now the revolutionary crisis of October 1917, and so on.[116]

---

[116] Hindess & Hirst, p. 322; cf. p. 323: "To say that the object of Marxist political theoretical analysis, the current situation, is constituted within political practice is not to surrender to the dictates of pragmatism. Marxist politics is only possible on the condition that it is based on theory, that its problems, programmes and practice are defined by and subject to the criticism of theory. This relation between theory and political practice is the essence of Marxism."

"The current situation" may, then, be defined as the current frontline of Marxist revolutionary strategy and practice at whatever point in time and space. One problematic aspect of bypassing historical analysis, which leaves us with only abstract theoretical analysis on the one hand and the analysis of "the current situation" on the other is that *agency* must be taken to be a crucial determinant in "the current situation", and historical development in general, so that a *direct* linking of the analysis of "the current situation" with abstract theoretical analysis means the exclusion of a major factor in the development of any "current situation", quite apart from historical development in general, in and from which "the current situation" inevitably develops, shaped by the interaction between social circumstances and agency which must be considered the motive power of historical development and transformations.

This has crucial implications for the analysis of "the current situation". Marx' *structural* analysis of *Capital* involves the conscious abstraction from agency, the (contrafactual) reduction of agents to "personifications of economic categories, supports of specific class relations and interests",[117] in order to isolate and analyse the developmental logic of the capitalist mode of production. As his description of the struggle over the normal working day,[118] his recognition that, unlike other commodities, the determination of the value of labour-power as a commodity involves a historical and moral aspect,[119] and his remark about "the absolute, general law of capitalist accumulation" that, "Like all other laws it is modified by manifold circumstances the analysis of which does not belong

---

[117] Marx, *Das Kapital*, 1, p. 16; cf. p. 100.
[118] Marx, *Das Kapital*, 1, ch. 8.6-7.
[119] Marx, *Das Kapital*, 1, p. 185.

here"[120] demonstrate, he was well aware of the distance between the analysis of the capitalist mode of production "so to speak on its ideal average"[121] on the one hand and historical analysis on the other.

Agency, human agents as the makers of their own history, "under the given and inherited circumstances with which they are directly confronted", and with the tradition of the dead generations weighing like a nightmare on the minds of the living,[122] and their articulation of their experiences of and responses to their "lived" reality, is a, indeed *the*, crucial cause of this distance. The actions of human agents, and thus the outcome eventuating from the interaction of their responses with each other and social circumstances cannot be *derived* from the developmental logic revealed by structural analysis, but cannot be fully accounted for without reference to this logic which is a co-determinant of social circumstances and the field of the possible in every "current situation". Hence, as argued in *Structure, Agency and Theory* and *Experience and Historical Materialism*,[123] the relationship between structural and historical materialism must be conceived as one of *complementarity* rather than continuity, "complementarity" being used in a sense similar to that of "The existence of different aspects of the description of a physical system, seemingly incompatible but both needed for a complete description of the system."[124]

---

[120] Marx, *Das Kapital*, 1, p. 673-674.
[121] Marx, *Das Kapital*, 3, p. 839.
[122] Marx, *The Eighteenth Brumaire of Louis Bonaparte*, p. 146 (*MEW*, 8, p. 115).
[123] Gram-Jensen, *Structure, Agency and Theory*, p. 490 ff; *Experience and Historical Materialism*, p. 152 ff.
[124] French & Kennedy, p. 370. Cf. Bohr, p. 74: "A most conspicuous characteristic of atomic physics is the novel relationship between phenomena observed under experimental conditions demanding different elementary concepts for their description.

If we define "the current situation" as the current frontline of Marxist revolutionary strategy and practice at whatever point in time and space,[125] it is of course true that it is irreducible to "an object given in the real, social reality at a given moment in time";[126] but it is *also* irreducible to "the political practice which constitutes it as an object":[127] it is part of the process of interaction between social circumstances and agency, and *neither* side: the objective social realities, or agents' articulation of their experiences of and responses to these realities, can be ignored if this situation is to be understood and the right strategy and tactics chosen and effectuated. "The current situation" is *present history* – part of the process of historical development. If we are to understand it, and *handle* it for our own purposes, including the transition from capitalism to socialism and eventually classless communist society, we must have a sufficiently realistic conception of what kind of process historical development is, and what possibilities and challenges "the current situation" offers us.

And yet Hindess & Hirst assert that, "Marxism, as a theoretical and a political practice, gains nothing from its association with historical writing and historical research."[128] For what reasons? A few comments on their argumentation to that effect, and on historical writing and historical research, are certainly relevant.

Indeed, however contrasting such experiences might appear when attempting to picture a course of atomic processes on classical lines, they have to be considered as complementary in the sense that they represent equally essential knowledge about atomic systems and together exhaust this knowledge."
[125] Cf. Hindess & Hirst, p. 322-323.
[126] Hindess & Hirst, p. 322.
[127] Hindess & Hirst, p. 322.
[128] Hindess & Hirst, p. 312.

c.

In *At the Limits of History*, Keith Jenkins writes that,

> In the 1980s I was becoming an adherent of the radical politics and political theory of Ernesto Laclau, out of which came a form of 'discursive Marxism' or 'post-Marxism', a Marxism influenced not least by Jacques Derrida and which had jettisoned the notion of historical inevitability whilst retaining key elements of Marxist method and political commitment. My reading of various texts by Paul Hirst and Barry Hindess (not least their *Pre-Capitalist Modes of Production* (1975)), wherein Marxist history had also been rejected, also influenced my move towards post-Marxism, whilst I had also become familiar with the 'cultural studies' and literary theory of Tony Bennett. In 1990 Bennett published his book, *Outside Literature*, in which, in chapters 2 and 3, he rejected Marxist history as teleology but kept a form of historical knowledge which I didn't think he needed to. And so I wrote this paper which was both respectful of Bennett yet critical of him insofar as I didn't think he took the rejection of history to its logical conclusions. Hindess and Hirst did do that, however, and I found their argument both logical – they indeed took their reasoning to its logical conclusion – and convincing. So in this paper I worked Bennett, Laclau, Hindess and Hirst together vis-à-vis my then embryonic notion that we were coming to a certain 'end of history' ... and that this was (probably) a good thing."[129]

We have, then, Jenkins' own words indicating the influence of Hindess and Hirst, particularly their *Pre-capitalist Modes of Production*, on the development of his ideas about history – an

---

[129] Jenkins, *At the Limits of History*, p. 22.

influence it is hard not to discern anyway when reading their conclusion to that book.[130] It seems worthwhile, then, to look a little closer at their argument on history, at least insofar as it is relevant in the context of Jenkins' postmodernist critique of it. To present it in their own words, for a start, a long quotation is necessary:

> The historian's conception of his object and his method of knowing is necessarily an empiricist one. The object of history is an object already given to knowledge. It is a given body of representations and a given finite body of real events which underlies those representations. This body of events and representations exists prior to any theory of it, its existence gives to the theory the object it must explain. The historian's theories are developed to account for this given. Theory and hypothesis must rationalise and explain this given object. A *scientific* history is the most complete and accurate saving of its phenomena. The given, the facts of history, is the measure of the explanations of it. Historical knowledge is limited to sifting the essential from the inessential among the facts, events and records given to it, and presenting an account which corresponds to the essential.

> History is condemned by the nature of its object to empiricism. Its object, the past, cannot be other than given, and given in one definite and unalterable modality. This object is supposed to have pre-existed its investigation and, as it no longer exists, it can in no way be transformed by this investigation. The double givenness of the object puts it beyond any modification of its conditions of existence, any variation of its forms by the operation of a knowledge. The given real

---

130 Cf. Perry, p. 111.

object has a finite and necessary character, definite events which no longer exist, and it exists in the mode of representation. No operation on the given representations can transform the real object of history for it is not present in them. Explanation is limited to finding reasons for what appears in the form of the representation. Despite the empiricist claims of historical practice the real object of history is inaccessible to knowledge. Even within empiricist philosophical epistemology it is recognised that historical knowledge is subject to severe limits. Positivist critics of the notion that history is a science have made much of these limitations. Even within the empiricist canons of knowledge it is recognised that there cannot be experimentation in history, that historical explanations are *post hoc* rationalisations, and that as historical phenomena are finite and unrepeatable, they cannot give rise to general laws.

There can be no escape from this empiricism. The object of history cannot be conceived as a theoretically constituted object, as an object not limited by what is given. Such a non-given object cannot be part of history; in being constituted theoretically it is constituted independently of the hitherto existing. History must conceive the object of its knowledge as a given object or cease to be historical. But this given real object, far from being real and given prior to investigation, is constituted by definite social and political ideologies. What the past *is* is determined by the content of the various ideological forms which operate within the parameters of historical knowledge. The content of the past, its nature, its periods and problems is determined by the character of a particular ideological form. The particular modes of writing history invest this or that body of representations with the status of a record. Artefacts, washing lists, court rolls, kitchen middens, memoirs, are converted into *texts* – representations through which the real may be read. The text, constituted as a text by its reading, is at the mercy of this reading. Far from working on the *past*, the ostensible object of history, historical knowledge works on a body of *texts*. These texts are a product of historical knowledge. The writing of history is the production of texts which interpret these texts.

The limitations of history are widely recognised, not least by sceptical historians. History is a potentially infinite text, constantly doubling back on itself, constantly being re-written. Marxist history in no sense escapes from these limitations. It cannot transform the conditions of the historian's practice without ceasing to be history, and if it respects these conditions then it must be merely another form of rationalising an object which it constitutes as the given. If Marxism gives us another history, if it recognises new representations as pertinent (the record of the class struggle, the aspirations of the masses, the evolution of material production, etc.), if it brings new ideological concerns to create, select and order the facts it will take as a given, then it merely gives us *another* history – a novel history, perhaps, but a history like all other histories.

It is the notion of a Marxist history, of a Marxism confined within conditions of the historian's practice, which is the contradictory enterprise. Marxism, as a theoretical and a political practice, gains nothing from its association with historical writing and historical research. The study of history is not only scientifically but also politically valueless. The object of history, the past, no matter how it is conceived, cannot affect present conditions. Historical events do not exist and can have no material effectivity in the present. The conditions of existence of present social relations necessarily exist in and are constantly reproduced in the present. It is not the 'present', what the past has vouchsafed to allow us, but the 'current situation' which it is the object of Marxist theory to elucidate and of Marxist political practice to act upon. All Marxist theory, however abstract it may be, however general its field of application, exists to make possible the analysis of the current situation.[131]

It is rather obvious what assertions in the quoted passages one might refer to in order to support Jenkins' rejection of history, including Marxist history:

[.....]. What the past *is* is determined by the content of the various ideological forms which operate within the parameters of historical knowledge. The content of the past, its nature, its periods and problems is determined by the character of a particular ideological form. The particular modes of writing history invest this or that body of representations with the status of a record. Artefacts, washing lists, court rolls, kitchen middens, memoirs, are converted into *texts* – representations through which the real may be read. The text, constituted as a text by its reading, is at the mercy of this reading. Far from working on the *past*, the ostensible object of history, historical knowledge works on a body of *texts*. These texts are a product of historical knowledge. The writing of history is the production of texts which interpret these texts.

[.....]. History is a potentially infinite text, constantly doubling back on itself, constantly being re-written.

---

[131] Hindess & Hirst, p. 310-312.

Marxist history in no sense escapes from these limitations.

The alternative Hindess & Hirst offer is an "abstract and theoretical" approach: "This book is a work of theory. Its approach is abstract and theoretical and it is concerned to determine the theoretical status and validity of certain specific concepts."[132] And as they argue on these concepts in the passages already quoted above:

> The field of application of these concepts is not history. We reject the notion of history as a coherent and worthwhile object of study. These concepts are abstract, their value is not limited by the analysis of the concrete. As concepts they can have a theoretical function even if concrete conditions to which they are pertinent do not exist, have not existed and will not exist. Concepts which are not used in the analysis of concrete conditions are not therefore speculative and empty. It is empiricism which conceives the necessary field of application of all concepts as the real. In fact concepts have a valid field of application *within theory*.

> The value of the concepts elaborated here is, indeed, predominantly *within theory*. There are certain concrete situations in which the concepts of the FMP, of primitive communism, and of the proof that there is no valid concept of AMP may be useful. For example, the proof that there is no concept of AMP may have value in demonstrating the illusions and the absurd political consequences which would follow from the attempt to use such a concept to analyse the social formations of contemporary Asia. This is a secondary matter. The primary value of the concepts elaborated here is in the

---

[132] Hindess & Hirst, p. 1.

rectification, elaboration and development of the concept of mode of production, and in clarifying the procedures by which the concepts of specific modes of production may be formed and proved. In particular we hope that this work will be of value in contributing to the formation of an anti-historicist theory of modes of production, a theory which avoids the pitfalls of Balibar's general theory. The urgent tasks of such a theory are the development of a concept of a capitalism dominated by finance capital, a concept which builds on and goes beyond Marx's concept of the CMP in which industrial capital is dominant, and the development of a rigorous concept of the socialist mode of production. If this work is of service in clarifying the way to these tasks then it will have justified itself.[133]

One obvious argument against Hindess & Hirst's dismissal of history is the fact that they argue about e. g. slave production in *historical* terms, adducing what they must consider historical *facts* against various views.[134] How can they meaningfully do so, if historical research and historical writing are mere (empiricist) exercises in ideology?[135] And, on the other hand, how *else* could they argue about the nature of modes of production if concepts of them are not to be mere figments of theory unrelated to any past or present reality?[136] And,

---

[133] Hindess & Hirst, p. 321-322.
[134] Hindess & Hirst, ch. 3, passim.
[135] Hindess & Hirst, p. 3, p. 311.
[136] Cf. Hindess & Hirst, p. 219: "Wittfogel distinguishes his method as: 'the use of big structural concepts for the purposes of identifying big patterns of societal structure and change' (*Oriental Despotism*, p. iii), and compares it to the method of Aristotle, Machiavelli and Adam Smith. We would prefer to call it empiricist speculation on a grand scale – the production of a generalised pseudo-description, in which empirical evidence features as exemplification and

finally, if all Marxist theory exists to make possible the analysis of the current situation, how can the applicability and relevance to that analysis of theoretical concepts, let alone those only pertinent to concrete conditions which "do not exist, have not existed and will not exist", be "a secondary matter"? The relevance of Hindess and Hirst's anti-empiricist, abstract and theoretical endeavour is rendered doubtful on their own assumptions.

The more substantial question of their critique of history remains, however. Is Hindess & Hirst's rejection of history justified, that is, is this description of the limitations of history actually correct? Or is it merely a caricature of what history is, or at least can be, that is, of what historians do, or at least what they can do? Before turning to this question, one may, however, note that if all Marxist history exists to make possible the analysis of the current situation, and this in its turn in order to make a difference to the course of historical development, then some knowledge about what *kind* of process that development is would seem relevant, and thus "Marxism, as a theoretical and political practice," it would seem, *has* something to gain from its association with historical writing and historical research, provided, of course, that it is able to produce such knowledge, which brings us back to the first question. *Are* historical writing and research inescapably empiricist? According to Hindess and Hirst,

> Empiricism represents knowledge as constructed out of 'given' elements, the elements of experience, the 'facts' of history, etc. Unfortunately for these positions facts are never 'given' to knowledge. They are always the product of definite practices, theoretical or ideological, conducted under definite real conditions. To

---

illustration, and where the generality described is an inexistent and ideological one."

pretend otherwise, to represent certain elements of knowledge as given in the real, is to denegate the central role of scientific practice, of experimentation and of explicit theoretical construction and argument, in the production of scientific knowledge. Facts are never *given*; they are always produced. The facts of the sciences are products of scientific practices. In the academic social sciences and history and also, it must be admitted, in the bulk of Marxist scholarship dealing with pre-capitalist societies the situation is quite different. The latter tends to be historical and descriptive in orientation and to treat the brief indications of, say, feudal or slave production in the works of Marx and Engels as more or less adequate descriptions of the structure of particular historical societies. The theoretical problem of the validity of the concept of a particular mode of production thus tends to be reduced to the empiricist problem of the correspondence between the concept and the 'facts' of history. For example, the problem of the validity of the conception of the 'Asiatic' mode of production tends to be discussed in terms of the 'facts' of Indian and Chinese history.

The empiricism of the academic social sciences and of much Marxist scholarship has serious theoretical effects. In so far as certain facts are represented as 'given' in the real or as 'given' by history they must fall below the level of theoretical determination: they cannot be the product of an explicit theoretical practice. The empiricism of these disciplines therefore ensures that these 'facts' are ideological constructs and that their 'theories' are, at best, sophisticated theoretical ideology.[137]

---

[137] Hindess & Hirst, p. 2-3.

For a start, the *relevance* of a theoretically constructed concept of the "Asiatic" mode of production in terms of accounting for, or making sense of, the history of certain societies would seem to depend quite considerably on the actual reality of the past of those societies. Hindess & Hirst refer to Althusser & Balibar, p. 34-40 for "the analysis of the empiricist conception of knowledge";[138] it is unnecessary to deal with the closed circle of Althusserian epistemology here. The relevant observation is that historical writing and research need not be as theoretically vacuous as Hindess and Hirst suggest. Historians may be perfectly well aware that historical evidence is in itself mute, and that it only speaks when interrogated in terms of a specific problematic informed by (more or less provisional) concepts and hypotheses. And that these concepts and hypotheses are themselves tested by their ability to aid the endeavour to *make sense of, account for*, the historical phenomena under investigation. Thompson has emphasised this *dialogue* between theory and evidence.[139] And noted that, "Self-generating hypotheses, subject to no empirical control, will deliver us into the bondage of contingency as swiftly – if not more swiftly – than will surrender to the "obvious" and manifest."[140]

Anderson has remarked that, "the past cannot be altered by any practice of the present. Its events will always be reinterpreted, its epochs rediscovered, by later generations; they cannot, in any sober materialist sense, be changed."[141] And while the past *as such*, in its *totality*, can never be reconstructed in historical writing, it is possible to ascertain various *aspects* of it, more or less plausibly, from the dialogue between theory

---

[138] Hindess & Hirst, p. 324 (note 1).
[139] Thompson, *The Poverty of Theory and Other Essays*, ch.s vi-vii, especially p. 37, p. 40.
[140] Thompson, *The Poverty of Theory and Other Essays*, p. 37; cf. p. 35, p. 124-125.
[141] Anderson, *Considerations on Western Marxism*, p. 110.

and evidence which may be questioned in many ways, *but the determinate properties of which do not allow it to be interpreted arbitrarily, and set limits to the questions in terms of which it is relevant.* And hence Hexter's argument on the practice of historians makes sense:

> [.....]. Historians and scientists both use footnotes, and for one purpose they use them in about the same way: they use them to cite to the 'literature' of the subject or problem about which they are writing. Historians, however, also use footnotes in a variety of other ways. One way historians use them and physicists do not is to cite to the historical record, the substrate of evidence on which historians erect their accounts of the past. Citation to that record is the way a historian makes his professional commitment clear in action, as the report on the experiment is the way a physicist makes his commitment clear. In both instances it is a commitment to maximum verisimilitude (which does not mean exact replication in every detail). For the physicist it is a maximum verisimilitude to the operations of nature as glimpsed through consideration of the experimental cluster; for the historian, verisimilitude to the happenings of the past as glimpsed through consideration of the surviving record.
>
> The well-nigh universal use of footnotes to the record by historians indicates that they are all still committed to writing about the past, as Ranke put it, *wie es eigentlich gewesen*, as it actually happened. In today's somewhat more sophisticated language, we might say that historians are concerned and committed to offer the best and most likely account of the past that can be sustained by the relevant extrinsic evidence. Let us call

this statement about the historian's commitment the "reality" rule.[142]

This should not be taken to mean that the evidence will speak for itself without being asked any specific questions, its transparent testimony gradually, as ever more evidence is dug up, coming together to form a likewise immediately transparent image of (aspects of) the past. As noted above, historical evidence only speaks when interrogated in terms of a specific problematic informed by (more or less provisional) concepts and hypotheses. And, given that it can be sustained by the relevant extrinsic evidence, whether an account of the past meeting that demand is the *best* and most *likely* one, is also a question of what is to be considered relevant and cogent by way of causal explanations. Our concepts, theories and views may be revised in the course of our dialogue with the evidence, or by direct critique of them, and our experiences more generally, but we are never approaching such evidence, or our "lived" reality, or "current situation", devoid of concepts, theories and views.

Our knowledge about the past must be considered incomplete, selective, approximate and provisional (in the sense that new evidence and experiences may conceivably prompt revisions), but nevertheless *real* if and insofar as it contains information about the past corresponding to aspects of the actual past. And while this can be tested against the evidence, such testing is not a matter of anything "given" to knowledge by this evidence, but of the interpretation and explanation of the evidence with its determinate properties by means of concepts and hypotheses, which are themselves tested in the course of this dialogue and modified or scrapped if they prove inadequate.

---

[142] Hexter, p. 54-55.

As for Hindess and Hirst's alternative, their "abstract and theoretical" approach, its distance from concrete history and "the current situation" is rather unmistakable. In fact, it seems to land them in a dead end comparable to that which they detect in Balibar: the inconsistency between the concept of modes of production which are self-reproductive and eternal because of structural causality on the one hand and that of transitional modes of society on the other.[143] More specifically, in the case of Hindess & Hirst a gap is established between theoretically and abstractly elaborated concepts of modes of production on the one hand, and "the current situation", forever receding into the past which is inaccessible to everything except "at best, sophisticated theoretical ideology."[144] What creates this gap is the absence of the *process* of historical development, the interaction between social circumstances and agency, and the *dialogue* between theory and evidence by means of which it is rendered intelligible. As Anderson argues, referring to Hindess & Hirst's position:

> [.....]. No responsible Marxism can either abdicate from the task of comprehending the immense universe of the past, or claim to exercise the jurisdiction of a material transformation of it. Marxist theory is thus not, despite every laudable temptation, to be equated with a revolutionary sociology. It can never be reduced to the 'analysis of the current conjuncture', in a now fashionable terminology. For by definition, what is current soon passes. To confine Marxism to the contemporary is to condemn it to a perpetual oblivion, in

---

[143] Hindess & Hirst, p. 275, p. 319-320. Cf. Balibar, "Self Criticism", p.59-60.
[144] Hindess & Hirst, p. 3.

which the present ceases to be knowable once it recedes into the past.[145]

There is, of course, nothing wrong with logical, conceptual analysis – quite the contrary; but there is *more* to historical development and transformations than conceptual logic – namely *agency*, including agents' articulation of their experiences of and responses to their "lived" reality, in specific, structurally *and* historically determined circumstances. If one starts from the – as argued above faulty – *premise* that, "What the past *is* is determined by the content of the various ideological forms which operate within the parameters of historical knowledge",[146] then abstract, theoretical logical conceptual analysis is of course what one is left with, with its potential and limits. But neither the articulation of theoretical concepts or that of experiences and responses takes place so to speak in the empty space. Readily as one may agree that, "All theoretical practice involves theoretical abstraction",[147] an obvious question is, "abstraction from *what?*"

Anticipating this question, Hindess & Hirst open their Conclusion as follows:

> We have no doubt that this book will appear to many people, historians and others, to be a contradictory enterprise. How can a book about pre-capitalist modes of production be abstract and anti-historical? Surely, the sole value of the concepts of the pre-capitalist modes of production is to serve as tools or research devices for the investigation of concrete historical

---

[145] Anderson, p. 110. As noted above, Hindess & Hirst are themselves reduced to adduce the historical facts they have rejected when arguing about past reality.
[146] Hindess & Hirst, p. 311.
[147] Hindess & Hirst, p. 3.

societies? What purpose do these concepts have if they are not used as guides to historical research?

Our answer to these questions is simple. They are based on a misrecognition, not only of the nature of our book, but of the nature of Marxist theory: a misrecognition which engenders a cosy conflation between Marxist theoretical work and the historians' practice, a misrecognition which reduces Marxist theory to historical method and to a philosophy of history. Marxism is not a 'science of history' and Marxist theoretical work has no necessary connection with the practice of the historian.[148]

But this postulate is definitely an inadequate answer to the question. Marx' analysis of *Capital* – which also makes use of historical material – is an effort to *make sense of* the capitalist mode of production, its social consequences and its social and historical tendencies (the direction in which it is pushing society), predicting its supersession brought about by the agency of the working class. An effort, that is, one aspect of which is the development and critique of concepts and theories related to the subject. And without some idea of the actual historical development – in the past and in the present – we simply cannot know, or test, what concepts, such as relations, forces and modes of production, exploitation and classes are relevant and important, and cannot have any idea of primitive communism, ancient or feudal modes of production, slavery as a system of social production, or the transition from feudalism to capitalism from which to elaborate their concepts by means of theoretical abstraction.

And as already mentioned, Hindess & Hirst deal, between their Introduction and their Conclusion, extensively with

---

[148] Hindess & Hirst, p. 308.

historical data and arguments, thus rendering their own position as inconsistent as that of Balibar on transitional modes of production which they (rightly) criticise:

[.....]. It is one thing to explain why any period of transition must come to an end; it is another to explain how periods of transition are possible. There is nothing in Balibar's theory of transitional and non-transitional modes of production to account for the movement from a mode of production that perpetually reproduces its conditions of existence to one that does not. This movement, and therefore the transition from one mode of production to another, is strictly unthinkable within *Reading Capital*'s Spinozist conception of the (non-transitional) mode of production. If transition is nevertheless to occur it can do so only at the price of theoretical incoherence. Even if transition is conceived as theoretically contingent, the result of accident, the effect of causes external to what *Reading Capital* represents as the Marxist theory of modes of production, it is clear that the very possibility of such contingency must be anathema to any Spinozist eternity.[149]

Hindess & Hirst postulate that historical evidence is at the mercy of the reading of it, and in effect that historical research and writing is merely an exercise in ideology. Nevertheless, they expressly challenge Wittfogel's thesis of "hydraulic society" using "empiricist criteria to challenge Wittfogel's empiricist pretensions",[150] and, citing historical data and historical writing by various authors throughout their chapters on pre-capitalist societies, they make the inconsistency even starker when, at a later point, they claim that,

---

[149] Hindess & Hirst, p. 275.
[150] Hindess & Hirst, p. 208; cf. ff.

[.....]. This implies not so much that the absolutist state is itself a transitional phenomenon but rather that the transition from feudalism to capitalism is possible only from the absolutist variant of feudalism. It is for this reason that the absolutist state is such a significant feature of the period of the development of capitalism in Europe. In addition it is well known that the intervention of the state played a major role in the struggle among European powers for the control of the world market opened up in the sixteenth and seventeenth centuries. Thus the question of the absolutist state and its connection with the development of capitalism is of the greatest importance for the whole of modern history.

Any extensive examination of this question would require a concrete analysis of the social formations of sixteenth- and seventeenth-century Europe which would be out of place in the present context.[151]

The inconsistency between this and Hindess & Hirst's insistence that historical research and writing are ideological and irrelevant, scientifically and politically valueless, and that

---

[151] Hindess & Hirst, p. 299; cf. p. 303: "Why is it that the commercial wars and the struggle of the European powers for control of the newly created world market play such a fundamental role in the period of the formation of capitalism?" And p. 307: "It is precisely in this double transformation that the displacement of dominance from the political to the economic level is effected. It follows that the commercial wars and struggles for control of the world market between the manufacturing states in the period of transition cannot be analysed without reference to the specific political transformations of the various states in this period."

history is no coherent and worthwhile object of study[152] is obvious. They introduced their project in this way:

> This book is a work of Marxist theory. Its object is to investigate the various pre-capitalist modes of production briefly indicated in the works of Marx and Engels and to examine the conditions of the transition from one mode of production to another. The fundamental concepts used in these investigations – the concepts of mode of production, of necessary-labour and surplus-labour, of politics and the state, and so on – are derived from *Capital* and from other works of Marxist theory. The aim of the analysis is to raise the conceptualisation of these modes of production and of transition to a more rigorous level. For each of the modes of production discussed in the book we attempt either to construct a general concept of that mode of production or else to show that such a general concept cannot be produced.[153]

Hindess & Hirst's argument is, then, in effect parasitical on Marx' analyses (which do make use of historical evidence) and *historical* accounts – which suggests the impossibility of dealing with the subject of pre-capitalist modes of production, or social analysis in general, without making use of historical (or other empirical) evidence and analysis, directly or indirectly, if there is to be any *substance* to the argument. Rejecting (methodically conscious) historical research, based on historical *criticism*, and its results as "at best, sophisticated theoretical ideology"[154] is to renounce the distinction between

---

[152] Hindess & Hirst, p. 311-312, p. 321.
[153] Hindess & Hirst, p. 1.
[154] Hindess & Hirst, p. 3.

ideas of past or present reality which are supported by evidence, and such that are not.[155]

Concepts and theories must live up to the demand for logical consistency; and elaborating concepts and theories, we can and must draw on, criticise and develop *existing* concepts and theories. But we must also systematise our current experiences of social reality and development, part of which is the application of concepts and theories to, and validating them against, these experiences. *And this must also involve historical material, whether on past or present reality*, critically examined and theorised to serve as material of such abstractions and concepts as embody our conceptions of historical development. For example, the *past* development of working-class struggles and organisations, and its causes, must be expected to offer valuable lessons and warnings. The (fleeting) "current situation" considered in isolation and worked on with abstract theoretical concepts cannot be assumed to offer a sufficient basis for the development of strategy and tactics. And obviously, for that matter, past outcomes of class struggles, and social development generally, will eventuate in fields of the possible different from those delimited by other outcomes which might have been. The present does not only recede into the past – it also eventuates from it.

Given this, and the more so as the irreducibility of agency as a determinant of historical development suggests that this development is an *open-ended* process, *both* structural *and* concrete historical analysis (including that of "the current situation") are blind unless considering – and directly or indirectly testable and tested against – historical reality/evidence. As Thompson has pertinently warned,

---

[155] Cf. Hexter's "reality" rule mentioned above, and Thompson's "Kangaroo Factor" cited below.

[.....]. There is a method of "theoretical practice" which I will describe as *The Kangaroo Factor*. We have noted long ago [.....] that this kind of idealism, since it prohibits any actual empirical engagements with social reality, is delivered, bound and gagged, into the hands of the most vulgar empiricism. That is, since it cannot know the world, the world must be assumed in its premises. And what is the world but the most vulgar manifestations and prejudices of "what everyone knows"?[156]

Thus, should "the procedures by which the concepts of specific modes of production may be formed and proved" not include analysis of the historical developments and variations of actual social formations dominated by them? Does the assertion that an urgent task is "the development of a concept of a capitalism dominated by finance capital which builds on and goes beyond Marx's concept of the CMP in which industrial capital is dominant" not point to a *historical* development (with, one may suppose, variations in time and space)? And to the inevitable interaction between historical development and knowledge *so far* on the one hand and theory, including abstraction and conceptual elaboration, on the other? Should "the development of a rigorous concept of the socialist mode of production" not be informed by the actual historical record of post-1917 "real existing socialism", in its global context?[157] And should not the struggle for socialism be informed by the historical record of the 19th, 20th and 21st centuries, including that global context too, and lessons from its progress, defeats and regression as well?

---

[156] Thompson, *The Poverty of Theory and Other Essays*, p. 124; cf. p. 35-36.
[157] See for the quoted problematics or tasks Hindess & Hirst, p. 321-322.

The fundamental fact that Marx' and Engels' expectations and predictions about the inevitable transition from capitalism to socialism and on to classless communist society have, so far, failed to come true is a historical one, and has to be accounted for in terms of the kind of process historical development is, and the actual history of advanced capitalist societies until now. The record obviously has to be analysed by means of theories and concepts developed in a dialogue with the evidence, but we cannot rely on abstract theoretical analysis *alone*. On the contrary, along with the record of post-1917 "real existing socialism", that of capitalism – in advanced capitalist formations and globally, and in the specific social formations – has to deliver the raw material from which theory and concepts can be developed and abstracted, and against which they may be tested.

As for the question about the *kind of process* historical development is, it has, for example, implications for the controversial conceptualisation of classes and their boundaries. This interdependence of theory and history may be illustrated as follows:

The Marxist debates on class analysis have to a large extent turned on *how* to define classes. Basically, two alternatives have been offered. The first one is to define classes in terms of *positions in the relations of production*. In advanced capitalist societies, this roughly means owners of capital (capitalists, bourgeoisie) as opposed to non-owners of means of production except their own labour-power which they are consequently forced to put up for sale (working class, proletariat); and, in addition, owners of their own labour-power *and* other means of production making up a third class, the petty bourgeoisie. The second one is to include other criteria such as functions in the process of production, power, role in relation to the maintenance of the social structure, ideological characteristics.

116

Erik Olin Wright has advanced six theoretical constraints on a general concept of classes:

1. Class structure imposes limits on class formation, class consciousness and class struggle.
2. Class structures constitute the essential qualitative lines of social demarcation in the historical trajectories of social change.
3. The concept of class is a relational concept.
4. The social relations which define classes are intrinsically antagonistic rather than symmetrical.
5. The objective basis of these antagonistic interests is exploitation.
6. The fundamental basis of exploitation is to be found in the social relations of production.[158]

Wright rejects such a definition as the one offered above, more specifically a definition of the working class as *non-owners of means of production except their own labour-power which they are consequently forced to put up for sale*. His argument for rejecting it is that it conforms to five out of the six restraints, but not the first one.[159] It is, in the first place, doubtful whether this is strictly speaking true. If "imposes limits on" is taken in the sense of Wright's own definition of *structural limitation*,[160] it means that the class structure delimits a field of the possible, with pressures and different degrees of probability, not, as Wright demands in *Classes*,[161] a category which may be considered uniform in its effects.

[158] Wright, *Classes*, p. 26-37.
[159] Wright, *Classes*, p. 38-39.
[160] Wright, *Class, Crisis and the State*, p. 15-16.
[161] Wright, *Classes*, p. 39.

More important, however, is the fact that the inclusion of other criteria (consciousness, function in the process of production, power, status or e. g. level of income) renders the analysis inconsistent, as such criteria cut across positions in relations of production and thus *overrule* them. This is most obvious in Poulantzas' class analysis, in which the working class, which is, according to him, "the only class that is revolutionary to the end",[162] is reduced to a minority by means of various economic and political criteria.[163] A class analysis based on relations of production must, therefore, be limited to this high level of abstraction if it is to be logically consistent.

Finally, the conception of historical development as *open-ended*, although within certain limits to the possible and hence not arbitrary, and the emphasis on agents' articulation of their experiences and responses, means that the position in a specific class cannot be *expected* to be uniform in its effects on agents' consciousness and class struggle. Within the limits determined by the relations of production and agents' positions in these, the development of agents' consciousness and class struggle will depend on the specific historical development, including the way the actors involved *handle* it. The actual development of classes, consciousness and class and other struggles can be *accounted for* in this context, but it cannot be *derived* from the class structure.

It would seem obvious that such a question cannot be settled without this dialogue between the elaboration of concepts and hypotheses, and logical analysis on the one hand, and historical knowledge (won by applying those analytical tools to the evidence, both they and historical knowledge being tested and corrected in the process) on the other. The conception

---

[162] Poulantzas, *Classes in Contemporary Capitalism*, p. 204.
[163] Wright, *Class, Crisis and the State*, p. 53-58.

of agents' articulation of their experiences of and responses to their "lived" reality as a central aspect of the process of historical development has a further implication, namely the assumption that,

> To what extent agents' experiences and responses correspond to their *objective interests* cannot be determined *a priori*. No inherent mechanism in the process of determination guarantees that they do, or that they do not. The specific ensembles of conditions for the articulation of experiences and responses obtaining for specific groups of agents (classes, fractions etcetera) will determine the limits and possibilities in this regard. Which is another way of saying that there is no guarantee that agents will necessarily *act on* their objective interests – or that they *never* will.[164]

This emphasises both the necessity of concrete analysis of "the current situation" and that of *historical* analysis, the two being, in fact, inseparable. What are the organisational, ideological and material resources[165] available to the class (and fractional etcetera) agents facing each other in the various struggles and fields in "the current situation"? How can working-class capacities, and in particular those of revolutionary-socialist organisations and movements, be augmented, and how can they be utilised optimally, and for what precise short- and long-term purposes? What such purposes should be adopted? Are various circumstances and developments historical variables changeable by conscious action, or are they inevitable consequences of the developmental logic of the dominant mode, or the type of society? What weaknesses and errors does the history of revolutionary socialism

---

[164] Gram-Jensen, *Structure, Agency and Theory*, p. 282; *Experience and Historical Materialism*, p. 144.
[165] Wright, Levine & Sober, p. 29.

and working-class organisations and struggles generally demonstrate? And how are they to be overcome?

The answers will certainly depend on structural analysis of the type of society and the dominant mode of production defining it, but also on that of the *specific* developmental phases and the *specific* social formations. And in both cases it will be necessary to use the kind of evidence which historians use, and to look into the past for causes of present social circumstances as well as raw material for *experiences* relevant, with all the necessary reservations and caution, for present struggles and questions (e. g. problems involved in either revolutionary-socialist, gradualist or reformist strategies, forms of organisation and action, etcetera) – and not to forget the interpretation and evaluation of inherited *theory*, which is in itself relying on evidence from the past: the texts in question, supplemented by, and read in the context of, the social reality in which they were written, and tested against that, and present reality.

In addition, one may ask what *relevance* the "empirical" material Lenin adduced "as the object of criticism or as a source of illustrations of a theoretical point"[166] has if it is not valid? And if the theoretical points are illustrated by it, does that not suggest that empirical factors actually *make a difference* in terms of the conditions for class struggle (problems and possibilities, strategic and tactical options)?

Hindess & Hirst do not, to be sure, deny that empirical factors make a difference, especially not as far as the reproduction or supersession of modes of production is concerned, but their presuppositions and definitions only makes their position more incoherent. They define a mode of production as "an articulated combination of relations and forces of

---

[166] Hindess & Hirst, p. 323.

production structured by the dominance of the relations of production. The relations of production define a specific mode of appropriation of surplus-labour and the specific form of social distribution of the means of production corresponding to that mode of appropriation of surplus-labour."[167] And as we have seen, this definition implies that,

> [.....]. Where, on the contrary, no set of corresponding productive forces can be deduced from a proposed mode of appropriation of surplus-labour, this latter belongs to no mode of production and cannot define a set of relations of production. We show in the chapter on the supposed 'Asiatic' mode of production that the concept of the appropriation of surplus-labour by the mechanism of tax/rent cannot define a set of relations of production since it belongs to no possible concept of an articulated combination of relations and forces of production.[168]

The notion or concept of the Asiatic mode of production is rejected because "this mode of appropriation of the surplus-product", by means of tax/rent, "corresponds to at least two distinct sets of forces of production: the forces entailed in independent peasant cultivation and communal cultivation."[169] No amount of historical evidence, then, that surplus-product has been appropriated in this way: a state apparatus which, as the owner of all land, imposes taxes or rents from the cultivators of land in social formations in which (at least) those two distinct sets of forces of production were found could, according to Hindess & Hirst's conceptualisation of a mode of production, support the idea of a mode of production (whether its designation as "Asiatic" is appropriate or

---

[167] Hindess & Hirst, p. 9-10.
[168] Hindess & Hirst, p. 11-12.
[169] Hindess & Hirst, p. 196.

not) defined by this mode of appropriation of surplus-labour: this is excluded by conceptual definition.[170]

This abstract and theoretical approach has a further consequence in terms of the relationship between theory and "the analysis of the current situation"; the passage which was quoted on the first page in section a. above states that,

> [.....]. Central to the concept of mode of production are the concepts of *reproduction* and *limit*. Entailed in the concept of reproduction is the persistence of the structure if its conditions of existence are secured – the concept of any mode of production must define the structure of that mode as one which makes a particular form of reproduction possible. The concept of *limit* specifies that the structure of a mode of production can only exist as a definite hierarchy of determinations, and that it exists as a totality only in so far as its structure in dominance and the form of action of that structure is preserved. Nothing in its concept prohibits the continued reproduction of a mode of production and nothing in its concept requires that a mode of production transgress its own limits, i.e. dissolve itself. It is because the concept of mode of production entails the concepts of reproduction and limit that the theory of transition is a theory limited to explaining the concrete conjunctures of transition between the dominance of one mode of production in a social formation and the dominance of another.[171]

---

[170] This is not to defend the concept of "the Asiatic mode of production", but to emphasise the fact that with another *definition* of a mode of production it might "have a valid field of application *within theory*." Hindess & Hirst, p. 321).
[171] Hindess & Hirst, p. 202.

In effect, the "theory of transition" seems, on this assumption, to amount to no more than the exclusion of the explanation of concrete conjunctures of transition from the realm of theory. In other words, Hindess & Hirst's approach creates the same gap between unhistorical theory on the one hand and untheorized concrete conjunctures on the other as became explicit in Balibar's "Self Criticism", in consequence of his conception of modes of production in *Reading Capital*: "the only real historical dialectic is the process of transformation of *each* concrete 'social formation' [.....] in reality they are the *only* object that is transformed, because they are the only one that really contains a history of class struggles."[172] *How* to account for, let alone *handle*, this history if approaching it on the assumption that "Marxism, as a theoretical and political practice, gains nothing from its association with historical writing and historical research" remains an unsolved puzzle.

The conclusion is that Hindess & Hirst's rejection of history as no coherent and worthwhile object of study must itself be rejected. Theoretical work enabling us to understand the process of historical development – in the past and/or the present – and *handle* it as effectively as possible is impossible without recourse to historical *evidence* – relating to the past and/or the present – from which to abstract concepts, problematics and answers. Evidence, to be sure, which must be sifted and tested in terms of its reliability and relevance, and interrogated according to problematics and concepts: *not*, that is, to be considered as immediately transparent, delivering immediately transparent answers of their own accord. But nor reducible to endlessly malleable material for any ideological interpretation one wants to impose on them: not reducible, that is, to something "constituted by definite social and

---

[172] Balibar, "Self Criticism", p. 59-60.

political ideologies", "at the mercy" of our readings of the past through it.[173] As Thompson puts it,

> Historical evidence has determinate properties. While any number of questions may be put to it, only certain questions will be appropriate. While any theory of historical process may be proposed, all theories are false which are not in conformity with the evidence's determinations. Herein lies the disciplinary court of appeal. In this sense it is true (we may agree here with Popper) that while historical knowledge must always fall short of positive proof (of the kinds appropriate to experimental science), false historical knowledge is generally subject to *dis*proof.[174]

Again, abstract theoretical elaboration (and testing in terms of logical consistency) of concepts cannot teach us any lessons about the actual historical conditions and practice of class struggle – such as for example those that may be drawn from Hickey's account of "The Shaping of the German Labour Movement: Miners in the Ruhr".[175] The lessons cannot simply be read from the evidence without thought, of course. But how can they be taken into account in the elaboration of concepts – and in "the analysis of the current situation" – if all historical knowledge is dismissed as mere ideology?

Historical knowledge is always incomplete, selective, approximate and provisional, but still substantiated, supported by evidence insofar as it has withstood the test of conformity with the determinations of the evidence. Without it, our theoretical work, the elaboration of concepts and theories, on

---

[173] Hindess & Hirst, p. 311.
[174] Thompson, *The Poverty of Theory and Other Essays*, p. 39-40.
[175] Cf. Gram-Jensen, *Structure, Agency and Theory*, p. 611-613; *Experience and Historical Materialism*, p. 158-161.

society and social development is simply blind, precisely reducible to any ideological construction, or discourse, we may arbitrarily choose to impose on it. Such constructions or discourses may be replaced by others at will, but they cannot be subjected to any test of their validity except in terms of purely logical consistency. The distance from Althusser's closed epistemological circle[176] to the relativism of Laclau & Mouffe and Jenkins is a short one.

And yet there is, after all, a distance, inasmuch as Althusser & Balibar are not postmodernists. Laclau & Mouffe argue on the postmodernist assumption that, "the truth, factual or otherwise, about the being of objects is constituted within a theoretical and discursive context, and the idea of a truth outside all context is simply nonsensical."[177] And Jenkins on what is basically the same assumption, namely that,

> [.....] we read the world as a text, and, logically, such readings are infinite. By which I do not mean that we just make up stories about the world/the past (that is, that we know the world/the past and then make up stories about them) but rather the claim is a much stronger one; that the world/the past comes to us always already as stories and that we cannot get out of these stories (narratives) to check if they correspond to the real world/past, because these 'always already' narratives constitute 'reality'.[178]

---

[176] Althusser and Balibar, p. 34, p. 67. Cf. Thompson's comments in *The Poverty of Theory and Other Essays*, p. 6, p. 21 ff.

[177] Laclau & Mouffe, "Post-Marxism without Apologies", p. 86; cf. p. 82 ff on their distinction between *being* of objects, which is discursively articulated, and their *existence*, which is not, but from which nothing follows (p. 91). And *Hegemony and Socialist Strategy*, p. 107-108.

[178] Jenkins, *Re-thinking History*, p. 11.

This assumption has been criticised in both *Structure, Agency and Theory* and *Experience and Historical Materialism*,[179] and there is no need to go through the arguments again in any detail. Apart from the fact that this fundamental assumption is merely an assumption or postulate, which is never really cogently *argued*, and that it is, like all such relativism, self-refuting, the idea that readings of texts, including the world/the past, are infinite is simply not true: if it were, all communication and hence all social life would break down/be impossible. It is significant that Hindess & Hirst, Laclau & Mouffe, and Jenkins, not only read and expound the texts of others without any reservations about the possibility of doing so, but also communicate their own views in the expectation that they will be able to get their points across to readers (why else bother?),[180] sometimes complaining that they have been misunderstood.[181] And despite Laclau & Mouffe's assertion about "truth" quoted above, and Jenkins' insistence, quoting Laclau, that "nobody has foundations",[182] they certainly

---

[179] Gram-Jensen, *Structure, Agency & Theory*, Part Two, ch. 4; *Experience and Historical Materialism*, essays 4-5.

[180] Laclau & Mouffe, "Post-Marxism without Apologies", p. 84, offers an explicit example, when they add to a statement that, "The reader who has followed our text to this point will have no difficulty in understanding why."

[181] "The second mistake Geras makes is that he reduces the discursive to a question of either speech, writing or thought, while our text explicitly affirms that, as long as every non-linguistic action is meaningful, it is also discursive." (Laclau & Mouffe, "Post-Marxism without Apologies", p. 85. Cf. Jenkins' assertion, in *At the Limits of History*, p. 89: "The understanding Perez Zagorin has of postmodernism and history – which he correctly thinks is typical of that held by most of his professional colleagues – is actually a misreading which deserves to be closely examined." No doubt about the possibility of identifying correct and incorrect reading of texts is visible here.

[182] Jenkins, *At the Limits of History*, p. 103, p. 241, p. 260.

argue on the assumption that their own relativistic position is more *true* than that of their opponents.

To conclude, we do not have to accept the idea that historical evidence does not impose limits to the valid ways in which it may be interpreted, that, "The text, constituted as a text by its reading, is at the mercy of this reading." This does not mean that it or the answers it may give to specific questions are simply transparent, or independent of theoretical context and elaboration, but that its properties exclude arbitrary interpretation by making the inconsistency of some interpretations with it demonstrable.[183] There is more to historical writing and research that ideological exercises, and the exclusion of historical knowledge from Marxist theory and practice is both unnecessary and damaging.

---

[183] As is argued at length against postmodernist critics of the historical discipline by Evans in his *In Defence of History*, especially ch. 4.

4. Human Agency.

[Slightly modified translation of a paper read on 16 March 2022 at a gathering in Copenhagen arranged by the Institute of Marxist Analysis]

Human Agency and Historical Development: Towards a Revised Historical-Materialist Approach.
First of all, a few words to introduce myself. I was born in 1953 and graduated from the University of Copenhagen as an MA in history and social studies in 1978. Like many others, I began to take an interest in historical materialism because of the commotion during the 1960s, and not least the war in Vietnam. At University, I consequently devoted considerable time to historical materialism in general and Marxist theory of the state in particular, at a time when the logic-of-capital trend and Althusserian structural Marxism were prominent in Denmark.

Apart from the general *theory of history*, this introduction to my book *Structure, Agency and Theory* will focus on the analysis of classes and the isolation of class struggle, which is also bound up with one of the fundamental problems dealt with in the book: whether the failure of Marx' and Engels' expectation of the inevitable transition from capitalism to socialism and eventually classless communist society can be accounted for within the framework of a Marxist historical materialism in a meaningful sense of that term.[184] For the sake of clarity, I will

---

[184] As observed in *Structure, Agency and Theory*, p. 18, abandoning any of the following assumptions will place a theory, paradigm or approach outside Marxist historical materialism in any meaningful sense of the term: 1. Social circumstances, including such as are due to agents' positions in relations of production, are determinants of agents' consciousness. 2. Capitalism is an exploitative, antagonistic, crisis-ridden and alienating mode of production. 3. The working class constituted by capitalist relations of production consequently

begin by summarising the following four basic notions mentioned in the Preface (p. 14) and taken up below:

1. The motive power of historical development and transformations is the interaction between social circumstances and agency constituting the actual process of historical eventuation.
2. Agents' responses to their "lived" reality (the ensemble of objective circumstances affecting them), and hence agency in the said interaction, depend on the *experiences* of their "lived" reality which agents articulate.
3. Historical determination must to a large extent be conceived of as the limitation of a field of the possible within which several outcomes may be possible and more or less probable.
4. Social theory must ultimately be judged by its ability to account for the actual historical record.

Structure, Agency and Theory was written throughout a period of twenty years since the day in the spring or summer of 2000 when, serving as an invigilator, I was struck by the difference it makes to history *that we act on what we think about the world and our possibilities rather than on the objective facts about them.* Prior to that moment there had been an extended period of work, still primarily on the problems of Marxist analysis of the *state*. The approaches of the logic-of-capital trend and that of Althusserian structuralist Marxism, both tending to reduce ideology and practice to effects of, respectively, the logic of capital and the social structure (and especially the conditions of reproduction of the latter), had proved to be useless. And the

---

has an objective interest in a transition from capitalism to socialism and eventually communism in the sense of a society based on the collective command of the means, process and outcome of production.

same was certainly true of the discourse-analytical approach conversely reducing both consciousness, social practice, historical development and, in effect, actors to discourse. On the other hand, that of the so-called *British Marxist historians* seemed empirically fruitful: capable of giving an account of the interaction between social circumstances and agency in the actual course of history, although without unequivocally suggesting any general theory of history.

The abovementioned thought was no doubt related to this unsolved problematic: structure, social practice and history. And to the recognition that the state and its actual functioning must be accounted for as part of the actual historical development and hence on the basis of *the kind of process this historical development is*. It is certainly also indebted to E. P. Thompson, who, in his critique of Althusser, emphasises *experience* as a fundamental concept.[185] But until the thought turned up, it remained obscure what the basis of a satisfactory answer might be.

The thought may seem trivial; but on Marx' assumption that human beings make their own history, although in given circumstances,[186] the implication is that the motive power of history is the interaction between social circumstances and agency.[187] To put it differently, if human beings were unable to anticipate something not yet in existence and work to bring it into existence,[188] there would not be any development of the productive forces, or any history of mankind – *unless* one postulates, in direct opposition to Marx' assumption, that history or some other objective, teleological mechanism imposes the thoughts and activity producing historical

---

[185] Thompson, 1978, p. 7; 1995, p. 9.

[186] Marx, *Der achtzehnte Brumaire des Louis Bonaparte*, p. 115.

[187] Sørensen, *Marxismen og den sociale orden*, p. 71 ff. Bosch, p. 222.

[188] Cf. Marx, *Das Kapital*, 1, p. 193.

development on human agents. If the notion of human agents as the makers of history is maintained, their articulation of their experiences of, and their responses to, their "lived" reality, and their resources or class capacities – "the organizational, ideological and material resources available to class agents"[189] – must be considered crucial factors. And if "history is *nothing* but the activity of man pursuing his aims",[190] this indicates an *open-ended* course of history.

However, if the motive power of history is *the dialectic of forces and relations of production*, it indicates a *closed* course of history. To be sure, Marx and Engels couple these two conceptions of historical development. They assume that the transition from one mode of production and type of society to another is accomplished by the class with an interest in the continued development of the productive forces. But in the 1859 Preface to *A Contribution to the Critique of Political Economy*, Marx suggests that, "No social order is ever destroyed before all the productive forces for which it is sufficient have been developed, and new superior relations never replace older ones before the material conditions for their existence have matured within the framework of the old society", and that mankind only sets itself such tasks as it is able to solve, because the task only presents itself when the material conditions for its solution are already present or at least in the course of formation.[191] *Firstly*, the question of class capacities is considered to be solved, or sure to be solved, here. And *secondly*, agency effectively tends to be subordinated to the dialectic of forces and relations of production, so that this dialectic, or history, is in effect using human agents as a means to its own aims.

---

[189] Wright, Levine & Sober, p. 29; cf. Levine & Wright and Wright, Levine & Sober, Part I, passim.
[190] Marx & Engels, *Die Heilige Familie*, p. 98; cf. *Die deutsche Ideologie*, p. 45.
[191] *MEW*, 13, p. 9.

This tendency is not taken to its logical conclusion by Marx or Engels (although certainly, in different ways, by the logic-of-capital trend and Althusser & Balibar's structural Marxism), but the tension in the historical materialism they have left to posterity is real.[192] And the conception of the dialectic of forces and relations of production as the motive power of historical development and transformations further implies the assumption that such transformations are assumed to occur when the relations of production turn into fetters on the development of the productive forces: it is assumed to be a law of history that the conflict between the productive forces and the capitalist relations of production will be solved by the transformation of the latter – and that this means the transition from capitalism to socialism and eventually classless communist society.

In *Enthüllungen über den Kommunistien-Prozeß zu Köln*, Marx writes that the working class will have to "go through 15, 20, 50 years of civil wars and popular struggles, not just to change conditions but to change yourselves and grow capable of political rule"[193] But in *Der Bürgerkrieg in Frankreich*, he writes that,

> The working class did not demand any miracles from the Commune. It has no pre-packaged Utopias to introduce by popular vote. It knows that to bring about its own liberation, and with that the superior way of living towards which contemporary society inexorably tends through its own economic development, it, the working class, has to go through long struggles, a whole series of historical processes, through which people as well as conditions are completely changed. It has no ideals to realise; it only has to liberate the

---

elements of the new society which have already developed in the womb of collapsing bourgeois society.[194]

In *Anti-Dühring*, it is emphasised that with the growing proletariat the capitalist mode of production is creating the power, which, under penalty of its own destruction, is forced to accomplish the transition from capitalism to socialism. And that by more and more forcing on the transformation of the vast means of production, already socialised, into state property, capitalism itself shows the way to accomplish this revolution: *"The proletariat seizes political power and turns the means of production in the first instance into state property"* – the state thus beginning to wither away.[195]

Theory, organisation and the development of class capacities are not irrelevant, and the birth pangs of the new society can be more or less protracted and hard.[196] But the eventual outcome is a foregone conclusion. That this conception is in fact found in Marx' and Engels' theoretical works, from *Die Heilige Familie* and *Die deutsche Ideologie* and onwards, should be sufficiently documented in *Structure, Agency and Theory* and *Experience and Historical Materialism*.

The conception of the dialectic of forces and relations of production as the motive power of historical development and transformations suffers from several weaknesses. *Unless* sufficient class capacities in the class with an interest in a historical transformation is assumed to be an *effect* of the dialectic, it cannot be taken for granted that a conflict between productive forces and relations of production triggers off an era of social revolution. And *if* it is *assumed* that sufficient class capacities *will* be present *when* such a conflict arises, this in effect

---

[194] *MEW*, 17, p. 343.
[195] *MEW*, 20, p. 261-262. Cf. *Die deutsche Ideologie*, p. 424.
[196] Cf. Marx, *Das Kapital*, 1, p. 15-16.

means that the dialectic, or history, is supposed to unfold according to a teleological-functionalist logic of which human actors are mere tools, *unless* one is able to offer a cogent non-teleological explanation of the development of the relevant class capacities.

In *Structure, Agency and Theory*, Part Four, ch. 1. d, it is demonstrated that Cohen's attempt to evade these problems[197] is unsuccessful.[198] More fundamentally we can only speak rationally about *intentions* or *purposes* of actors, or, if you like, creatures with (a certain degree of) *consciousness* – not of e. g. structures, modes of production or history. If we try to avoid to make what is effectively the postulate that structures, modes of production or history have consciousness, intentions or purposes by means of the assertion that they have effects *corresponding to* those they would have *if* they were ruled, or ruling, by intentions or purposes, that history develops *as if* it moves towards an inherent *telos*, we must demonstrate, firstly, that its course actually fits in with that assertion, and, secondly, *why* (in that case) it does so, in normal terms of cause and effect.

In addition, it seems hard to fit capitalism and its history into the model of development sketched in the 1859 Preface. The working class has tended to be divided and class struggle to be isolated rather than the class being educated, united and organised by the capitalist process of production as predicted by Marx in *Das Kapital*, 1, p. 791. And it seems doubtful whether the development of the productive forces is, in the real sense of the word, *fettered* by capitalist relations of production. Marx argues persuasively that to a great extent their development on the conditions imposed by capitalism forms a contrast to the potential for satisfying human needs which

---

[197] Cohen, ch. IX-X.
[198] Cf. Rigby, p. 294 – and Cohen himself, p. 341.

is due to the pressure for technological development exerted by these very same conditions.[199] But one would hardly be right in saying that capitalism is not sufficient for the development of more productive forces.

Both in the first section of the *Manifesto* and in *Das Kapital*, 1, ch. 24.7 (where the conclusion to section 1 of the *Manifesto* is quoted in a note), the assertion of the inevitable transition from capitalism to socialism is made in continuation of accounting for the corresponding transition to capitalist production from precapitalist production, with *its* barriers to the development of the productive forces. The barriers imposed by *capitalism* to that same development are now expected to be overcome by the bursting of its capitalist integument.[200] It is a reasonable assumption that the conception of the dialectic of forces and relations of production as the motive power of historical development and above all historical transformations is based on the impression of the industrial revolution. But it cannot be said to rest on any longer historical perspective, and an analysis in depth of other historical transformations. Hence it is a probable hypothesis that Marx and Engels advance a general explanation of historical transformations on an inadequate basis: the pressure for development of the productive forces exerted by the capitalist mode of production, and the contrast between capitalist and precapitalist societies in this regard. The weakness of this explanation is also confirmed by the distance between their prediction and the actual historical development since the beginning of the 20th century – not least as regards working-class consciousness and politics.

---

[199] Marx, "Rede auf der Jahresfeier des "People's Paper" am 14. April 1856 in London".
[200] Marx, *Das Kapital*, 1, p. 791.

The conclusion to be drawn is that the conception of the dialectic of forces and relations of production as the motive power of historical development and transformations should be replaced by the conception of the interaction between social circumstances and agency as the motive power of history. And hence by the notion of historical development as a process which is *open-ended* – within certain limits.

In terms of practice this may not make all that much of a difference, as the accomplishment of the transition from capitalism to socialism will in any event require the organisation of a majority around this objective, and the right strategy for its realisation. But *firstly*, no *guarantee* that the transition *will* indeed be accomplished is assumed. And *secondly*, a *credible* strategy, *both* for the transition *and* for the organisation of an *effectively* classless society, must be worked out: *partly* recognising the fact that there is no basis for the assurance in the 1859 Preface that the dialectic of forces and relations of production drives history towards this society, which leaves a strategic gap in Marx' and Engels' historical materialism; and *partly* considering the experiences with post-1917 "real existing socialism". Among other things, this is discussed in the final fourth part of *Structure, Agency and Theory*, unfortunately, but as to be expected, without arriving at any practical solution to the problem.

Social Circumstances and Agency.
What is left, then, is the conception of the interaction between social circumstances on the one hand and agency, human practice, on the other as the motive power of history. In *Structure, Agency and Theory* (p. 1327), agency is defined as:

> **actors'** relating to, and handling, their **"lived" reality**, practice through which they respond to this reality rather than acting merely as its **supports**; it involves the articulation of both their **experience** of "lived" reality,

a more or less close approximation to its actual nature, and their **response** to it, that is their choice of some course of action according to their experience of "lived" reality, including their notions of legitimate and realistic options. Agency has both a cognitive and an emotional (as well as a strategic) aspect, and responses to (the experience of) "lived" reality may be either rational or irrational.

Here, I will firstly consider *experience* as a central fundamental concept, and then its implications in terms of the analysis of *classes* and, lastly, *the isolation of class struggle* and the analysis of *"the welfare state"* to demonstrate the empirical relevance of this approach.

In *Structure, Agency and Theory* (p. 280-283) and *Experience and Historical Materialism* (p. 141-145), 15 main assumptions about experiences and responses are listed. At this point, only the two first and the last need to be quoted:

1. What is denoted as the articulation of experiences and responses is, in the final analysis, the articulation of *consciousness* and *social practice*.
2. The articulation of experiences is in fact an integral part of agents' responses to "lived" reality, inasmuch as answers to the question: "who are we, what is our situation, what can and should be done about it?" are articulated in and as experience.
15. The suggested conception of the interaction between social circumstances and agency implies an element of *unpredictability* in the process of historical development. In the first place, actors are able to learn from experience and hence modify their responses

accordingly.[201] Secondly, insofar as the range of possible responses delimited by the ensemble of identifiable determinants is not down to one, several responses may eventuate, with different effects on the actual outcome. And thirdly, *novel* (or more precisely intrinsically new)[202] experiences and responses may be articulated. All of this means that the actual development may be accounted for, but cannot be predicted except with various degrees of uncertainty. *History is open-ended, though not arbitrary.*

We respond to our social situation as articulated in our experience – which is not given to us as a reflection of the situation as it objectively is, but precisely articulated by *us* on certain structurally and historically determined conditions, including ideological struggle – with non-uniform resources – to influence it, and with social *practice* as the acid test of consciousness and responses – what Thompson has termed the *dialogue* between social being and social consciousness.[203]

The question asked in the context of assumption 2: "who are we, what is our situation, what can and should be done about it?", is crucial, because actors' notion of and response to their

---

[201] Cf. Carr, *What Is History?*, p. 70-71: "One reason why history rarely repeats itself among historically conscious people is that the dramatis personae are aware at the second performance of the denouement of the first, and their action is affected by that knowledge." By way of illustration, he adds that, "The Bolsheviks knew that the French revolution had ended in a Napoleon, and feared that their own revolution might end in the same way. They therefore mistrusted Trotsky, who among their leaders looked most like a Napoleon, and trusted Stalin, who looked least like a Napoleon."
[202] Cf. Popper, p. 10, for the distinction between intrinsic newness and novelty of arrangement.
[203] Thompson, 1978, p. 9; 1995, p. 12.

social position and existence depend on the way they answer it: *what* class or other group they belong to, *what* its relation to others is, to *whom* they owe solidarity or are opposed, *what*, if anything, it is realistic and legitimate to do about the situation of group and individual – change it, defend it, or passively accept it. And it cannot be taken for granted that the answer is self-evident – the actors in question have to *work it out*, with the information and the ideational tools they have or can acquire or develop. In this regard it is probably realistic to consider the articulation of experiences and responses on the one hand and social theory on the other as a continuum rather than polar opposites. And in this context, capitalism with its "mute compulsion" and opaque mechanism of exploitation may be said to pose specific challenges. Without entering into details on the isolation of class struggle – its limitation to such forms as do not objectively threaten to disrupt the type of society and the dominant relations of production – at *this* point, there are ideological and practical possibilities to keep the struggles over interests in capitalist societies within such limits. In terms of consciousness, the only limitation is that ideologies to that end must appear *meaningful* to agents in their given situations to have an attraction for them.

The Analysis of Classes.

With the sketched conception of the process of history as a backdrop, the implications in terms of the analysis of *classes* and *class struggle* in capitalist societies can now be outlined. The Marxist debates on class analysis have to a large extent turned on *how* to define classes. Basically, two alternatives have been offered. The first one is to define classes in terms of *positions in the relations of production*. In advanced capitalist societies, this roughly means owners of capital (capitalists, bourgeoisie) as opposed to non-owners of means of production except their own labour-power which they are consequently forced to put up for sale (working class, proletariat);

and, in addition, owners of their own labour-power *and* other means of production making up a third class, the petty bourgeoisie. The second one is to include other criteria such as functions in the process of production, power, role in relation to the maintenance of the social structure, ideological characteristics.

Erik Olin Wright has advanced six theoretical constraints on a general concept of classes:

1. Class structure imposes limits on class formation, class consciousness and class struggle.
2. Class structures constitute the essential qualitative lines of social demarcation in the historical trajectories of social change.
3. The concept of class is a relational concept.
4. The social relations which define classes are intrinsically antagonistic rather than symmetrical.
5. The objective basis of these antagonistic interests is exploitation.
6. The fundamental basis of exploitation is to be found in the social relations of production.[204]

Wright rejects such a definition as the one offered above, more specifically a definition of the working class as *non-owners of means of production except their own labour-power which they are consequently forced to put up for sale*. His argument for rejecting it is that it conforms to five out of the six restraints, but not the first one.[205] It is, in the first place, doubtful whether this is strictly speaking true. If "imposes limits on" is taken in the sense of Wright's own definition of *structural limitation*,[206] it means that the class structure delimits a field of the possible,

---

[204] Wright, *Classes*, p. 26-37.
[205] Wright, *Classes*, p. 38-39.
[206] Wright, *Class, Crisis and the State*, p. 15-16.

with pressures and different degrees of probability, not, as Wright demands in *Classes*,[207] a category which may be considered uniform in its effects.

More important, however, is the fact that the inclusion of other criteria (consciousness, function in the process of production, power, status or e. g. level of income) renders the analysis inconsistent, as such criteria cut across positions in relations of production and thus *overrule* them. This is most obvious in Poulantzas' class analysis, in which the working class, which is, according to him, "the only class that is revolutionary to the end",[208] is reduced to a minority by means of various economic and political criteria.[209] A class analysis based on relations of production must, therefore, be limited to this high level of abstraction if it is to be logically consistent.

Finally, the conception of historical development as *open-ended*, although within certain limits to the possible and hence not arbitrary, and the emphasis on agents' articulation of their experiences and responses, means that the position in a specific class cannot be *expected* to be uniform in its effects on agents' consciousness and class struggle. Within the limits determined by the relations of production and agents' positions in these, the development of agents' consciousness and class struggle will depend on the specific historical development, including the way the actors involved *handle* it. The actual development of classes, consciousness and class and other struggles can be *accounted for* in this context, but it cannot be *derived* from the class structure.

---

[207] Wright, *Classes*, p. 39.
[208] Poulantzas, *Classes in Contemporary Capitalism*, p. 204.
[209] Wright, *Class, Crisis and the State*, p. 53-58.

As a last aspect of the problem of class analysis, attention should be drawn to the distinction introduced in *Structure, Agency and Theory* between, on the one hand, the fundamental *class* interests, which are definable from the abstract analysis of the mode of production: the interest of the exploiting class in maintaining the given mode of production as opposed to the interest of the exploited class to abolish that mode and thus the exploitation it is subjected to. And, on the other hand, the actual *historical* structure of interests which has to be defined at the level of historical analysis (p. 387 ff.). *And* to the 13th main assumption about experience and responses:

> To what extent agents' experiences and responses correspond to their *objective interests* cannot be determined *a priori*. No inherent mechanism in the process of determination guarantees that they do, or that they do not. The specific ensemble of conditions for the articulation of experiences and responses obtaining for specific groups of agents (classes, fractions etcetera) will determine the limits and possibilities in this regard. Which is another way of saying that there is no guarantee that agents will necessarily *act on* their objective interests – or that they *never* will.[210]

The Isolation of Class Struggle.

With this, a basis for understanding the historical phenomenon which has, with a term borrowed from Poulantzas,[211] been labelled *the isolation of class struggle*,[212] has been established. As mentioned above, it denotes the limitation of agents' responses to such forms as do not objectively threaten to disrupt the capitalist type of society and its dominant relations

---

[210] *Structure, Agency and Theory*, p. 282; *Experience and Historical Materialism*, p. 144-145.

[211] Poulantzas, *Political Power and Social Classes*, p. 130.

[212] *Structure, Agency and Theory*, Part Three, ch. 1.

of production. Apart from the historical fact that downright *repression* has also contributed to counteracting the organisation of the working class around its fundamental interest in the transition from capitalism to socialism and classless communist society, this *effect of isolation* may be caused by one or more of the following circumstances:

1. That agents do not realise they are members of the working class.
2. That they do not see the antagonism between capital and labour.
3. That they do not perceive the nature of this antagonism and hence the preconditions for doing away with it.
4. That they do not consider a revolutionary transformation *possible*.
5. That the working class is split into fractions etcetera in such a way as not to be united around its fundamental interest.
6. That the struggle to realise this fundamental interest is waged as a struggle for measures that are actually no threat to capitalism (gradualist and other illusory strategies for transcending capitalism).

The first three points refer to the not immediately transparent capitalist mechanism of exploitation, the first one also, like the fifth one, to the consequently not immediately transparent class structure of capitalist societies. To put it differently, nor is there any immediately transparent answer to the question: "who are we, what is our situation, what can and should be done about it?" The struggle for a better position may, quite apart from appeals to "national" identity and "national" solidarity, be waged as *class* struggle, with a revolutionary-socialist or reformist horizon, but also as *fractional, group* or *individual* struggle for a better position in the given social hierarchy, e. g. by means of the educational system. It is not without reason that Poulantzas emphasises the *competition* among wage-earning workers.[213] For that matter, Marx and Engels mentioned it as well, but in a more optimistic vein, in the *Manifesto*: "This organisation of the proletarians into a class, and consequently into a political party, is continually being upset again by the competition between the workers themselves. But it ever rises up again, stronger, firmer, mightier."[214]

In *Structure, Agency and Theory*, Part Three, ch. 1, a number of older and newer examples of the *hierarchisation* of the working class are offered. For one thing, this hierarchisation contributes to the ability of bourgeois parties to attract members of the class. For another, it is reflected by Poulantzas' exclusion of large groups of wage-earners from the class, and his definition of so-called mental workers as belonging to the petty bourgeoisie according to the politico-ideological criterion that, "in their place within the social division of labour they maintain political and ideological relations of subordination of the working class to capital (the division of mental and manual labour), and because this aspect of their class determination is the dominant one."[215]

As far as the isolation of class struggle is concerned, one may conclude that the expectation Marx and Engels expressed in the *Manifesto* has hitherto proved too optimistic. The competition among workers has historically also manifested itself as the phenomenon Parkin has labelled with Weber's term *social closure*: the more or less systematic and successful attempt of various groups to monopolise favourable positions and thus better conditions of work and pay, status etcetera.[216] The

---

[213] Poulantzas, *Political Power and Social Classes*, p. 130.

[214] Marx & Engels, *Manifest der Kommunistischen Partei*, p. 471.

[215] Poulantzas, *Classes in Contemporary Capitalism*, p. 242.

[216] Parkin, p. 44.

exclusion of potential competitors may be by means of examinations ("meritocracy") or by criteria of nation (language), ethnicity, religion, "race" or gender. It is obvious that this phenomenon counteracts solidarity in, and organisation of, the working class; but also, that however repulsive it is, especially in its extreme and violent forms, it *makes sense* as a strategy for the struggle of fractions and other groups for a favourable position in existing hierarchies. As Mau has observed, Marx was aware of the competition between Irish and English workers,[217] and the persistence of the phenomenon in the USA have e. g. been emphasised by Baran & Sweezy.[218] Incidentally, German Nazism may be considered an extreme example with its ugly combination of nationalism and racism (*and* sexism).

There is probably no need to say much about the fourth point, but it does suggest the ideological strength the capitalist social order derives from the mere fact of *being* the actually existing social order – as well as, of course, the lack of a credible strategy for the transition to socialism and classless communist society. The sixth one points very directly to the isolation of class struggle: the distinction it refers to is that between a *revolutionary-socialist* strategy, a *gradualist* one aiming at the transition to socialism and communism by means of gradual measures, and a *reformist* one aiming at reforms within the capitalist framework.

The weakness common to the two last-mentioned ones is that, *as long as* capitalist production is vital to the material reproduction of society, the state is forced to function in a way compatible with the continuation of this production and hence the maintenance of the mute compulsion of capitalism

---

[217] Mau, p. 301-302. Marx, "Der Generalrat an den Föderalrat der romanischen Schweiz", p. 388-389.
[218] Baran & Sweezy, ch. 9.

and the power of the owners of capital to reduce material production and thus force the state and/or the working class to retreat. And, in the case of reformism, that reforms won by the working class will always be liable to be rolled back if, or when, the economic and political conjunctures become less favourable, which is likely to happen, given the unequal economic, ideological and political resources and the capitalist crises. As far as the revolutionary-socialist strategy is concerned, this *structural determination of the state* underlines the necessity of a realistic strategy for the transition from capitalist to socialist production at a sufficiently high level, partly to maintain support for the transition, partly to be able to defend it effectively against resistance by violent means – from within and/or without.

Therborn has pointed out that while *the development of bourgeois democracy* may well be *made possible* by the purely economic nature of capitalist exploitation which does not presuppose an unequal politico-juridical status of exploiter and exploited, it is *in actual fact* the result of the *contradictions* of capitalism – and pressure *from below*. The same may be said about "the welfare state". The need for higher wages and better conditions of work, for organisation to be able to fight effectively for them, for measures against the consequences of unemployment, old age, sickness, invalidity and the loss of a breadwinner are easy to articulate as experience for most sellers of labour-power. And the same goes for the need for political influence if such needs are to be met. At the same time ever increasing productivity makes it possible to meet them within the framework of the capitalist economy. On the other hand, bourgeois actors may learn that compromising can be less dangerous than confrontations – and that votes are a (necessary) means of acquiring influence for bourgeois parties too.[219] The British Conservative Party's accept of "the welfare state" after its

---

[219] *Structure, Agency and Theory*, Part Three, ch. 6.

electoral defeat in 1945[220] may be considered an example of actors' adaptive strategic response to the political conjuncture they have experienced.

It seems obvious that party structures and political frontlines are influenced by the conflicting fundamental *and* historical interests in capitalist societies – and by disagreements about the strategies for *handling* them. At the same time, it has to be recognized that ideological and political conflicts are *irreducible* to effects of the structure of classes and fractions.

A functionalist explanation of the development of "the welfare state" cannot account for the differences between the liberal, the conservative-corporate and the social-democratic varieties of it analysed by Esping-Andersen, and its different history of development in different countries. It is probably also significant that the social-democratic variety has done better than the two others in terms of reducing poverty.[221] And one may add that an explanation of the historical clout of reformist politics in terms of the *sense* it has made to working-class actors is preferable to one which, in Adam Przeworski's words, makes the working class appear as "a perpetual dupe of ideological domination, or, at best, as repeatedly betrayed by its leadership."[222]

With the necessary caution, one may conclude that the conception of the interaction between social circumstances and agency as the motive power of historical development and transformations seems to have a good explanatory power with regard to empirical history. This is confirmed by the fact that e. g. both the British Marxist historians (Hobsbawm,

---

[220] *Structure, Agency and Theory*, Part Three, ch. 5. b. Addison, passim.
[221] Goodin et al., p. 154-162.
[222] Przeworski, p. 202. Poulantzas, *Fascism and Dictatorship*, p. 151, offers an example in terms of ideological domination.

Thompson, Dobb, Hilton, Hill) and Evans, Curt Sørensen and Piketty have contributed cogent historical accounts and explanations based on an analogous approach.[223]

One may add that the relationship between structural and historical analysis must be considered *complementary* in the sense that between them, they require the consideration of aspects which are seemingly incompatible but both needed for a complete analysis.[224] The actual interaction between social circumstances and agency in capitalist society cannot be accounted for without understanding the developmental logic of the capitalist mode of production. But whereas the endeavour in *Das Kapital* is to elucidate this logic "on its ideal average"[225] by means of abstracting from agency, the (contrafactual) reduction of agents to "personifications of economic categories, supports of specific class relations and interests",[226] agents *transcend* this role as bearers in the actual process of historical development, so that another mode of analysis and explanation is required here.

In this context it is significant that Marx touches the limit of structural analysis in his analysis of the struggle over the normal working day[227] and with his accentuation of the fact that, in contradistinction to other commodities, the determination of the value of labour-power involves a historical and moral aspect.[228] The same is obviously enough true when, considering "the absolute general law of capitalist accumulation", he notes that like all other laws it is "modified in its eventuation by manifold circumstances the analysis of which does not

---

[223] Explicitly articulated by Sørensen in *Den europæiske deltagelseskrise*, p. 70.
[224] *Structure, Agency and Theory*, p. 490.
[225] Marx, *Das Kapital*, 3, *MEW*, 25, p. 839.
[226] Marx, *Das Kapital*, 1, p. 16; cf. p. 100.
[227] Marx, *Das Kapital*, 1, Kap. 8.5.
[228] Marx, *Das Kapital*, 1, p. 185.

belong here."[229] It is *not* a mere matter of moving continually from the (abstract) structural analysis to the (concrete) historical analysis by adding ever more details to the picture, but one of the difference between a developmental logic and mode of explanation involving only agents reduced to character masks on the one hand, and on the other hand an interaction and mode of explanation involving them precisely as *actors*, who *experience* their *concrete* social reality and respond to it, that is, *handle* it in accordance with their experiences. Which means that some of the more or less probable possibilities present in the specific situation are realised rather than others.

The supports of the character masks of capital are under the mute compulsion of capitalism to accumulate capital, but they have to find out *how*, in specific structurally and historically determined conditions and without any guarantee that the line of action they choose is optimal, or even realistic. The third main assumption about experience and responses is that the experience articulated by agents indirectly or directly spells out their *horizon of action*, which must be distinguished from their *objective range of options*[230] – a distinction which is of course also relevant in the context of the isolation of class struggle. The conception of the interaction between social circumstances and agency as the motive power of historical development and transformations does not in itself provide answers to the problems involved in the development of a revolutionary-socialist strategy, but paves the way for a more realistic discussion of them. As mentioned in the Introduction to *Structure, Agency and Theory* (p. 28), this will be a collective task within several theoretical fields – also including the interpretation of *future* historical experience.

---

[229] Marx, *Das Kapital*, 1, p. 674.
[230] *Structure, Agency and Theory*, p. 280; *Experience and Historical Materialism*, p. 142.

5. In Defence of *Structure, Agency and Theory.*

a. Determinism and Objective Interests.

There is one general and one specific point of criticism in the first review of *Structure, Agency and Theory* to appear,[231] at least as far as this writer is aware, which merit comment. To start with the general one, the reviewer complains that, "too often there are long series of quotations the aim of which is to prove that the presented reading is correct", which should have been weeded out by an editor.

The reason for these numerous and often lengthy quotations, and the knowledge that they make the reading more cumbersome is found on p. 45-46 in the book, towards the end of the Introduction:

> Whenever various contributions in or outside the Marxist tradition are criticised, an endeavour is made to provide adequate substantiation and argument. While this undoubtedly renders the book more cumbersome than it might otherwise have been, it seems necessary to do so in order to avoid the kind of aridly dismissive polemic so sadly familiar in and about Marxism, and to enable readers to form a well-founded judgment.[232]

---

[231] For this review, by Reinout Bosch, see: marxistiskanalyse.dk/2022/02/05/anmeldelse-structure-agency-theory/.

[232] Gram-Jensen, *Structure, Agency and Theory*, p. 45-46 (referred to as *Structure, Agency and Theory* in the notes below). Cf. Draper, *Karl Marx's Theory of Revolution*, I, p. 20-21 on this method with its "serious literary disadvantages" but "so clearly demanded in the interest of simple scholarship [.....]. The method, apparently so "academic" is in fact directed to the possibility of objective verification, "so that the reader may form and independent opinion.""

The specific point of criticism is put forward in the very first lines following the caption: "The book contains a series of interesting points, but Ib Gram-Jensen falls into the very determinism he wants to dispose of." The explanation comes in the penultimate paragraph:

> This explanation of various ideological positions, in its turn based on the chapter on class analysis, suffers from the peculiar weakness of assuming that the working class has an objective interest in socialism. Of course, some pages are dedicated to the question. But I am not convinced that it tallies credibly with Ib Gram-Jensen's emphasis that history must be understood as the interaction of social structure and human beings' lived experience. Instead, it seems a conscious relapse into the determinist view of the past.

This statement is a little baffling. Indeed, it only seems to make any sense at all on the assumption that the idea of an objective working-class interest in socialism implies the expectation that the working class *will* at some point in time effect a transition from capitalism to socialism and eventually classless communist society – an expectation of Marx and Engels repeatedly and explicitly refuted in *Structure, Agency and Theory*, where "objective interests" are defined in this way:

> [.....] the realisation or maintenance of a state of "lived" reality directly or indirectly making it more likely that agents experience (a higher degree of) gratification or avoid experiencing the opposite is in their objective interest – whether experienced as such or not.[233]

And the definition of the "determinism" rejected in the text goes:

---

[233] *Structure, Agency and Theory*, p. 1331.

[.....] the determinism ascribed to Marx in the present text denotes the belief that some long-term terminus of human (pre-)history or the development of capitalism, such as a transition to socialism and eventually communism, can be predicted with certainty. The term itself has other meanings as well.[234]

The same definition is in fact offered in the Introduction[235] and in the second paragraph of Part One, ch. 2:

To avoid any misunderstanding, the word "determinism" is used in the non-derogatory sense defined above in the Introduction, denoting the belief that some long-term terminus of human (pre-)history or the development of capitalism, such as a transition to socialism and eventually communism, can be predicted with certainty."[236]

As for the acting on objective interests in the sense of the definition quoted above, one of the main assumptions about agents' experiences and assumptions presented in the book goes:

---

[234] *Structure, Agency and Theory*, p. 1328.

[235] *Structure, Agency and Theory*, p. 22, note 12: "It should perhaps be stated at this point that in the present text *and* the said appendix, "determinist" or "determinism" are simply terms used to describe and denote, respectively, the belief that some long-term terminus if human (pre-)history or the development of capitalism, such as a transition to socialism and eventually communism, can be predicted with certainty – e.g. because it is made inevitable from the objective dynamic of capitalist accumulation, or from the way human actors can be assumed to respond to their social circumstances."

[236] *Structure, Agency and Theory*, p. 103.

To what extent agents' experiences and responses correspond to their *objective interests* cannot be determined *a priori*. No inherent mechanism in the process of determination guarantees that they do, or that they do not. The specific ensemble of conditions for the articulation of experiences and responses obtaining for specific groups of agents (classes, fractions etcetera) will determine the limits and possibilities in this regard. Which is another way of saying that there is no guarantee that agents will necessarily *act on* their objective interests – or that they *never* will.[237]

So, the idea that the notion of an objective working-class interest in socialism amounts to a relapse into determinism is absurd. As for the idea of objective interests itself, it is hard to disagree with Erik Olin-Wright that, for example, "People certainly have an 'objective interest' in increasing their capacity to act."[238] And that,

> [.....]. Marx certainly regarded class interests as having an objective status, and the issue here is what it is about those relations that might justify such a claim. The assumption is that people always have an objective interest in their material welfare, where this is defined as the combination of how much they consume and how hard they have to work to get that consumption. There is therefore no assumption that people universally have an objective interest in *increasing* their consumption, but they do have an interest in reducing the toil necessary to obtain whatever level of consumption they desire. An exploitative relation necessarily implies either that some people must toil more so that others can toil less, or that they must consume

---

[237] *Structure, Agency and Theory*, p. 282.
[238] Wright, *Classes*, p. 28.

less at a given level of toil so that others can consume more, or both. In either case people universally have an objective interest in not being exploited materially, since in the absence of exploitation they would toil less and/or consume more. It is because the interests structured by exploitation are objective that we can describe the antagonisms between classes as intrinsic rather than contingent.[239]

It would seem to take a rather far-fetched philosophical argument to refute the idea that working-class agents would be better off in this sense if liberated from the mute compulsion of capitalist relations, if, being liberated from exploitation, free to choose to consume more and/or to toil less, and free to decide on their own fate within the limits imposed by their metabolism with nature, collectively and individually. Just as it would seem trivial that agents are actually better off with food enough rather than starving, with comfortable housing rather than inadequate housing or homelessness, or living under rule of law rather than the arbitrary exercise of power, etcetera, etcetera.

The critique in the review is the more baffling as Bosch has written, with a reference to Wright, Levine & Sober, that,

> [.....]. Therefore, we have to emphasise that the emergence of collective actors with interests in transforming relations of production which are fettered only explains the transformation of the relations if these actors have a capacity to pursue their interests effectively.[240]

---

[239] Wright, *Classes*, p. 36.

[240] Bosch, p. 119. The reference is to Wright, Levine & Sober, p. 39: "The emergence of collective actors with interests in transforming the relations of production under conditions of fettering explains transformation of the relations only if those actors also have

Even if a systematic search in Bosch's own book has not been made, there are certainly passages in it which make his criticism seem strange. On p. 15, for example, we find the sentence: "This discussion leads to a first treatment of the interests of human beings as a motive power of development [*menneskets interesser som en drivkraft i udviklingen*]." On p. 90, divisions of interests between the groups making up a class are mentioned. On p. 94, we find the words, "If a class wants to fight for or defend its interests". On p. 155, Bosch suggests that, "The working class is the first one really producing in common and come together in large units of persons with common class interests." And on p. 190, he argues that,

> [.....]. It is a fundamental materialistic position that interests, ideas and convictions are not the same thing. The ruling ideas in a society are different throughout the social formations. They are the attempts of people to understand their own situation. As bridge building between faith and knowledge. It is precisely such ideas which prevent the realisation of objective interests until the point at which a crisis breaks out in the structure underlying such ideas.

The Marxist concept of exploitation is explained,[241] and Bosch is certainly ready to write of classes and their interests;

---

a capacity to pursue their interests effectively." It may be noted in passing that Bosch gets the meaning of the sentence he translates into Danish wrong, as the words "under conditions of fettering" in Levine, Wright & Sober of course refer to relations of production fettering the development of the productive forces, not these relations themselves being fettered. A similar error of translation is found in the review, where he quotes a passage in *Structure, Agency and Structure*, p. 195.
[241] Bosch, p. 84 ff.; cf. p. 261-262.

but what does he mean by *objective* interests? The answer is suggested a couple of pages later:

In his attempt to distinguish between interests and people's self-perception, Bosch seems to conclude that actors' interests come into being at the intersection between their *objectives* and *obstacles* to their realisation: "Through the encounter with the obstacles the common interest in overcoming them comes into being."[242]

This definition does in fact suggest a concept of "objective" interests in a sense different from that defined in *Structure, Agency and Theory*: insofar as common interests in overcoming obstacles to objectives of actors have come into being, they may be considered "objective" in the sense of actually existing. But firstly, this does not explain how the idea of objective interests in the sense defined in *Structure, Agency and Theory* implies a relapse into determinism.[243] And secondly, in effect Bosch's conception of interests seems hard to distinguish from Laclau & Mouffe's discourse-analytical one:

> [.....]. Ours is a criticism not of the notion of 'interests' but of their supposedly *objective* character: that is to say, of the idea that social agents have interests of which they are not conscious. To construct an 'interest' is a slow historical process, which takes place through complex ideological, discursive and institutional practices. Only to the extent that social agents participate in collective totalities are their identities constructed in a way that makes them capable of calculating and negotiating with other forces. 'Interests', then are a social product and do not exist independently of the

---

[242] Bosch, p. 192; cf. p. 190-196.
[243] And in spite of making that criticism, Bosch asserts that classes "necessarily oppose each other" (p. 261).

consciousness of the agents who are their bearers. The idea of an '*objective* interest' presupposes, instead, that social agents, far from being part of a process in which interests are constructed, merely recognize them – that is to say, that those interests are inscribed in their nature as a gift from Heaven. [.....] Again, we are not dealing with an 'either/or' alternative. *There are* interests, but these are precarious historical products which are always subjected to processes of dissolution and redefinition. What there are not, however, are *objective* interests, in the sense in which they are postulated in the 'false consciousness' approach.[244]

The only difference between Laclau & Mouffe's "interests" in the sense described in that passage on the one hand and Bosch's "objectives" on the other is their different designations. The differentiation between objectives as such on the one hand and interests defined as coming into being through the encounter between these objectives and the obstacles to their realisation allows Bosch to refer to objective interests without logical inconsistency, but those interests are only "objective" in the sense of existing *insofar as* the relevant objectives and obstacles do. The question whether given actors will *actually* be better off if some objective is realised (that is, if their interest in overcoming the obstacles to its realisation is realised), or whether they would have more to gain by pursuing some *other* objective, is sidetracked. If, taking Bosch at his word, workers do not articulate the transition from capitalism to socialism and eventually classless capitalist society as an objective, they do not have an interest in overcoming the obstacles to that transition either.

---

[244] Laclau & Mouffe, "Post-Marxism without Apologies", p. 96-97. Cf. for a critique of their position and arguments *Structure, Agency and Theory*, Part Two, ch. 4.

In fact, on p. 133 an answer to the question about Bosch's conception of interests is found – not, to be sure, in the shape of an actual definition of interests (objective or not), but in that of the following consideration on progress, which is indeed inconsistent with that of objective interests in the sense suggested in *Structure, Agency and Theory*:

> [.....]. Progress is an abstract expression which cannot be bound by anything but our subjective evaluation in the light of our own lifetime. Human beings' concrete objectives arise from time to time through the process of history, not from some external source. To understand progress, one must understand it as a process into which every historical period fills its own content. Progress can only be understood as an objective we set ourselves in the future, and towards which we can ascertain that historical processes have moved.[245]

A problem with this conception is that while Marx' and Engels' conception of the dialectic of the forces and relations of production as the motive power of historical development and transformations would certainly point towards the idea of the transition to socialism and eventually classless communist society as progress from a working-class, and in the final analysis a generally human, perspective (which might well become the actual objective of the majority of people in capitalist societies), Bosch posits that "we" set ourselves the objective defining progress in the future. Who are "we" in a class society, if classes have different objectives and hence different interests in terms of social/historical development, and the progress of some may mean the ruin of others?[246]

---

[245] Bosch, p. 133; cf. p. 16.
[246] Bosch, p. 128-129.

The only logical conclusion from this is that "we" in a meaningful sense of that word setting objectives and realising them according to our notions of progress or "the good life" *presupposes* the collective command of the means, process and outcome of production defining classless communist society. *Collective* because otherwise there would be no "we" able to transcend the limiting of given progress to some rather than all inherent in the existence of classes,[247] and *command* because the realisation of whatever objectives set requires effective control of social development even if these objectives are indeed realisable.

It is significant in this context that Marx does not (as a kind of proto-Fukuyama) predict the end of history as the consequence of the supersession of capitalism; on the contrary, he declares that the end of capitalism is the end of the *pre*history of human society.[248] In other words, the history proper of mankind begins with the transition to classless society. No class divisions or mute compulsion of the economic relations stop the members of this society from setting themselves the objective they consider embodies the optimal collective progress achievable in the given objective circumstances, or from reconsidering it if it seems unachievable or less than optimal.

If this argument is valid, the working class *does* have an objective interest in a transition from capitalism to socialism and

---

[247] That is, the precondition for the future situation envisaged by Bosch is in effect the transition envisaged by Marx and Engels in the *Manifesto*: "In place of the old bourgeois society, with its classes and class antagonisms, we shall have an association, in which the free development of each is the condition for the free development of all." (Marx & Engels, *Manifest der Kommunistichen Partei*, p. 482. Cf. Engels, *Anti-Dühring*, p. 335-336 (*MEW*, 20, p. 264) on the leap of man from the realm of necessity to the realm of freedom).

[248] Marx, *A Contribution to the Critique of Political Economy*, p. 22 (*MEW*, 13, p. 9).

eventually communism in the sense of a classless society based on the collective command of the means, process and outcome of production. In addition, one may consider the notion that the members of this class, taken as a body, will experience a higher degree of gratification without capitalist or any other exploitation, and with increased capacity to act, plausible enough to maintain it.

What is the consequence? In *Structure, Agency and Theory*, it is argued that abandoning any of the following the assumptions is inconsistent with the claim to argue within anything describable as a historical-materialist or Marxist framework or the Marxist tradition in any meaningful sense of those terms:

1. Social circumstances, including such as are due to agents' positions in relations of production, are determinants of agents' consciousness.
2. Capitalism is an exploitative, antagonistic, crisis-ridden and alienating mode of production.
3. The working class constituted by capitalist relations of production consequently has an objective interest in a transition from capitalism to socialism and eventually communism in the sense of a classless society based on the collective command of the means, process and outcome of production.[249]

Bosch has in effect abandoned the third assumption, substituting agents' given objectives for objective interests derivable from agents' social circumstances, whether or not agents are actually conscious of them.[250] But if this assumption is abandoned (which is rather inconsistent if the second is

---

[249] *Structure, Agency and Theory*, p. 18.
[250] Arguing such interests will, admittedly, involve assumptions about human beings' nature and needs, but, as Wright's arguments quoted above show, only rather trivial assumptions.

retained), historical materialism is effectively reduced to an approach to historical analysis: if we are left with nothing but given objectives the validity of which cannot be questioned in any meaningful way, the very idea of superseding capitalism is rendered meaningless.

b. The Process of Historical Development.

What kind of a process is historical development as conceived of in *Structure, Agency and Theory*? It is, in the first place, described as "an open-ended process of eventuation",[251] a process which, in the course of eventuating, delimits the field of the possible, with pressures and probabilities, within which its subsequent development eventuates; and a process the motive power of which is the interaction between social circumstances and agency, with agents' articulation of their experiences of and responses to their "lived" reality (the objective circumstances in which agents live, whether conscious of them or not: the total ensemble of objective conditions affecting the life of agents). What is meant by this may be outlined as follows:

The possible in terms of the structure of actually existing *social formations* will be delimited by the dominant *mode of production* (defined by specific *relations of production*) defining the *type of society* to which the social formation in question belongs, constituting a specific variety of this type. The mode of production/the social structure defining it will not be found in its pure form, derivable from its defining relations of production, in the actually existing social formation, but in its interaction with, and with its actual development and forms affected by, other (non-dominant) modes of production and geographically, climatically and historically determined

---

[251] *Structure, Agency and Theory*, p. 1037-1038. The argument in this section dealing specifically with the nature and unpredictability of history draws on *Structure, Agency and Theory*, Part Four, ch. 1. f.

circumstances (technological, institutional, ideological etcetera) – structure and these factors interacting at any specific point in time and space with human *agency*: agents' articulation of their experiences of and responses to their "lived" reality, manifesting themselves in agents' *practice*, and the effects of the interaction between this and social circumstances on historical eventuation.

This eventuation resulting from the interaction between social circumstances and agency means the delimitation of a specific field of the possible, with specific pressures and probabilities, within which the interaction between social circumstances (thus modified) and agency continues to eventuate in another specific delimitation of the possible, with specific pressures and probabilities, and so on, historical development thus, in its very process of development, producing its own historically specific conditions within structurally and historically determined limits to the possible which cannot be assumed to allow only *one* specific outcome. While this does not, of course, exclude or eliminate constant factors such as physical laws, human beings' biological make-up and needs etcetera, it leaves the process of historical development *open-ended* inasmuch as its precise future course and outcomes are not predictable from its state at a given point in time.

This peculiar nature of this social and historical process of interaction between social circumstances and agency: that it is neither simply arbitrary or non-causal, nor predictable, is emphasised in *Structure, Agency and Theory*: agents' articulation of their experiences of and responses to their "lived" reality, and thus the outcome of the process is impossible to predict precisely. Hence the process is "chaotic" in the sense of its outcome at any given point in time and space being explainable after the event (provided the relevant data are available), but impossible to predict with certainty,[252] although the type of society and the identifiable social circumstances delimit the field of the possible, with identifiable pressures and probabilities.[253] The process of historical development is thus, in its actual form, the realisation of some possibilities rather than others in an open-ended process within certain (structurally and historically determined) limits to the possible, and, within those limits, open-ended in terms of its future course.

This outline of the conception of the process of historical development is suggested in *Structure, Agency and Theory.*

[252] Cf. Hobsbawm, *Age of Extremes*, p. 541-542: "Chaos theory helped to put a new spin, as it were, on old causality. It broke the links between causality and predictability, for its essence was not that events were fortuitous but that the effects which followed specifiable causes could not be predicted. It reinforced another development, pioneered among palaeontologists, and of considerable interest to historians. This suggests that chains of historical and evolutionary development are perfectly coherent and capable of explanation *after* the fact, but that the eventual results cannot be predicted from the outset, because, if the same course was set again, any early change, however slight and without apparent importance at the time, 'and evolution cascades into a radically different channel' (Gould, 1981, p. 51)."

[253] Cf. Wright, *Class, Crisis and the State*, p. 14-15 on *"Structural Limitation*: This constitutes a pattern of determination in which some social structure establishes limits within which some other structure or process can vary, and establishes probabilities for the specific structures or processes that are possible within those limits. That is, structural limitation implies that certain forms of the determined structure have been excluded entirely and some possible forms are more likely than others. This pattern of determination is especially important for understanding the sense in which economic structures "ultimately" determine political and ideological structures: economic structures set limits on the possible forms of political and ideological structures, and make some of those possible forms more likely than others, but they do not rigidly determine in a mechanistic manner any given form of political and ideological relations."

According to this conception, it is possible to analyse the limits to the possible, probabilities and various possibilities and conditions at various points in time and space (i. e. historical conjunctures), but the future course and outcomes of historical development cannot be derived from any set of *laws* appliable to the given conditions obtaining in the conjuncture: they remain irreducibly open-ended, although more or less well-informed, conscious endeavours to turn them into some specific direction must indeed be considered possible.

c. Meikle.

In the course of the discussion after a lecture delivered by this writer in March 2022 on *Structure, Agency and Theory*,[254]

> It was likewise, citing Scott Meikle (*Essentialism in the Thought of Karl Marx*), submitted that one has to have an eye for what is tendencies in a development, and what is accidental occurrences. Perhaps, it was suggested, the relationship between the development of the productive forces and human agency should be seen with this eye. That is, that the development of the productive forces is a partly foreseeable tendency, whereas human agency will always be unpredictable.
>
> Especially the frequently adduced quotation from the *Manifesto*:

---

[254] marxistiskanalyse.dk/2022/03/20reportage-og-video-mennesket-som-aktoer/ (visited 15 March 2022). The wording of the quoted passages has been slightly modified at some points in order to render the meaning as clear as possible in English. The quotation in the text is from Marx & Engels, *Manifest der Kommunistischen Partei*, p. 462. Cf. Ib Gram-Jensen, *Experience and Historical Materialism* (referred to as *Experience and Historical Materialism* in the notes below), p. 71-73 for the "chain of argumentation of some length" leading to the conclusion.

> Freeman and slave, patrician and plebeian, lord and serf, guild-master and journeyman, in a word, oppressor and oppressed, stood in constant opposition to one another, carried on an uninterrupted, now hidden, now open fight, a fight that each time ended, either in a revolutionary reconstitution of society at large, or in the common ruin of the contending classes.

lead to a more history-centred discussion focusing on the open and dual potentiality Marx sketches for the general development. Either by means of one class overthrowing the other, or through common ruin. Thus, it was argued, the climate crisis might well become the ruin of our civilisation, with no communist revolution occurring. Gram-Jensen was manifestly activated at this point, and defended his position to the effect that the same text ends with the conclusion that the fall of the bourgeoisie and the victory of the proletariat are equally inevitable, inferred from a chain of argumentation of some length, so that the passage could not be explained away as mere agitation.

Meikle was cited in support of the suggestion that Marx' predictions should be read (in an Aristotelean, teleological-essentialist sense) as indications of developmental *tendencies*, which may or may not be realised, rather than unqualified predictions about what is bound to happen.[255] This writer has not, it should be noted, read Meikle's book, nor does he intend to do so, or deal with it in the present context. This

---

[255] By way of illustration, a caterpillar, for example, has the potential to develop into a butterfly, but will not *necessarily* realise this *telos*: many caterpillars perish before they become butterflies.

disinclination is not due to arrogance,[256] but to the fact that *only* the abovementioned interpretation of Marx' predictions in support of which that of Meikle was cited, is at issue here. The point is that this interpretation of Marx (and Engels), whether based on a correct reading of Meikle or not, is demonstrably untenable as a reading of Marx' (and Engels') actual words in such texts as *Die deutsche Ideologie*, the *Manifesto*, the 1859 Preface to *A Contribution to the Critique of Political Economy*, *Capital* and *Anti-Dühring* – and, of course, Marx' and Engels' explicit rejection of teleology in *Die Heilige Familie* and *Die deutsche Ideologie*,[257] and their words about Darwin's *The Origin of Species* having finished off, or dealt a deathblow to, teleology.[258]

Moreover, the fact is that while Marx did indeed state that "the absolute, general law of capitalist accumulation" is "like all laws" modified in its eventuation by concrete circumstances,[259] he made no similar reservation as to the inevitability of the transition from capitalism to socialism and eventually classless communist society:

> The essential condition for the existence, and for the sway of the bourgeois class, is the formation and augmentation of capital; the condition for capital is wage labour. Wage labour rests exclusively on competition between the labourers. The advance of industry, whose involuntary promoter is the bourgeoisie,

---

[256] A contributary cause is that the book does not seem to be available in the Danish library system, and the exorbitant price of buying it abroad and having it sent from there.

[257] Marx & Engels, *Die heilige Familie*, p. 98; *Die deutsche Ideologie*, p. 45.

[258] Engels, "Engels an Marx in London 11. oder 12. Dezember 1859". Marx, "Marx an Ferdinand Lasalle in Berlin, 16. Januar 1861", p. 578.

[259] Marx, *Das Kapital*, 1, p. 674.

replaces the isolation of the labourers, due to competition, by their revolutionary combination, due to association. The development of modern industry, therefore, cuts from under its feet the very foundation on which the bourgeoisie produces and appropriates products. What the bourgeoisie therefore produces, above all, are its own grave-diggers. Its fall and the victory of the proletariat are equally inevitable.[260]

If we are to accept that Marx meant "possible" when he wrote "inevitable" [*unvermeidlich*], we must assume that he (and likewise Engels) deliberately and consistently expressed himself in code. To the best knowledge of this writer, no evidence supporting that idea has ever been produced. And while one may certainly argue that Marx and Engels *should* have considered the supersession of capitalism by socialism and eventually communism a *possibility* rather than the inevitable outcome of the dialectic of forces and relations of production which they considered the motive power of historical development and transformations,[261] there is nothing to suggest that they did so, although several authors have asserted that they did not consider that supersession inevitable.[262] Moreover, there are few references to teleology in *MEW*;

---

[260] Marx & Engels, *Manifest der Kommunistischen Partei*, p. 473-474. Cf. for other examples Marx, *Das Kapital*, 1, p. 790-791. Engels, *Anti-Dühring*, p. 188-189 (*MEW*, 20, p. 146-147), and Part III, ch. II. Others are quoted in *Structure, Agency and Theory*, Part One, ch.s 2-3, and Appendix Three.

[261] Most famously stated by Marx in his 1859 Preface to *A Contribution to the Critique of Political Economy*, p. 20-22 (*MEW*, 13, p. 8-9).

[262] See for this *Structure, Agency and Theory*, Part One, ch.s 2-3 and Appendix Three, and the second essay in *Experience and Historical Materialism*.

Herferth lists a total of 14,[263] and insofar the relevant passages register any opinion of Marx or Engels about teleological views, it is negative.

The point would seem to be that we should take Marx and Engels at their word, and read them straightforwardly – except when a really good reason not to do so can be demonstrated – rather than try to avoid untenable predictions in their texts by reinterpreting their statements and concepts retrospectively. Such an attempt can only lead to arbitrary readings. If the interpretation suggested in the course of the discussion were to be accepted as correct, the suggested sense of essence, potential and teleology must have left some demonstrable traces in Marx' texts. Or, to put it another way, reading Marx' texts according to that interpretation would have to make demonstrably better sense of these texts, eliminate tensions and contradictions, or, one might say, "anomalies" left in them by other readings.

Instead, the suggested "Aristotelian" reading *leads to* "anomalies" or "puzzles": why does Marx not explain that he is making predictions in the suggested sense of *potentiality* rather than inevitability? Why, more specifically, does he *write* "inevitable" if he *means* "potential"? And why does he *explain* the inevitability of historical transformations, according to the conception of the dialectic of forces and relations of production as the motive power of historical development and transformations in his letter to Annenkow[264] and elsewhere? Or assert that all the difference agents can make in this context is that of shortening or alleviating the birthpangs? Or warn Germany that it is bound to go through a development

---

[263] Herferth, p. 841, "Teleologie": **2**, p. 83; **3**, p. 45, 159; **20**, p. 61, 315, 466, 479, 518; **27**, p. 57; **29**, p. 524; **30**, p. 578; **32**, p. 203; **E.1**, p. 56-57, 588.
[264] "Marx an Pawel Wassiljewitsch Annenkow in Paris, 28. Dezember [1846]", p. 549; cf. *Das Elend der Philosophie*, p. 140-141.

similar to that of Britain? Not to mention the words about laws of transition he approvingly quotes in the afterword the 2nd edition of *Capital*?

Finally, one is entitled to ask, where is the *evidence* suggesting that Marx (and Engels) only insisted on the inevitability of the supersession of capitalism by socialism and eventually classless communist society for the sake of agitation? There are a number of references to and quotations from Aristotle in Marx' and Engels' texts,[265] but none of them suggest that the supersession of capitalism is only considered a potentiality which may not be realised. Nor is that suggested in any of the passages in which Marx and Engels, in their central texts, mention this supersession – indeed, to the best knowledge of this writer nobody has ever produced such evidence. And unless *convincing* evidence to this effect is produced, we have to read their predictions in a literal sense, to take them at their word.

To state the decisive point again: if the suggested "Aristotelian" influence of Aristotle on Marx is a fact, this fact must be taken to be legible from Marx' texts. The *only* evidence that could demonstrate that Marx only considered the

---

[265] In one letter, Marx actually names Aristoteles as his favourite ancient philosopher (Marx an Ferdinand Lasalle in Düsseldorf, 21. Dezember 1857", p. 547; cf. *MEW*, Ergänzungsband, Schriften bis 1844, erster Teil, p. 61: Marx' admiration for Aristotle is a documented fact). On the other hand, while there are numerous references to, and comments on, Aristotle in this volume of *MEW*, in Marx' doctoral thesis and his preparatory studies for it, there is nothing supporting the idea that his later predictions about the supersession of capitalism should be read to the effect that it is merely a potentiality. In the *Grundrisse*, there are actually two references to potentiality (p. 91, p. 134), the second one with an explicit reference to Aristotle, both in contexts unrelated to historical transformations.

supersession of capitalism by socialism and eventually class-less communist society a potentiality in the Aristotelian sense would be passages in these texts which can most cogently be read to that effect; and there are no such passages, but several the most cogent reading of which is to the opposite effect: that this supersession is inevitable.

To the best knowledge of this writer, the only passage which might, *on the face of it*, be interpreted as expressing something like the idea of potentiality cut short by historical contingency is the one quoted above from the opening of the *Manifesto*. The meaning of "the common ruin of the contending classes" is, however, made clear by one in *Die deutsche Ideologie*: in the case of some societies in the past, the potential for historical transformation as the consequence of internal class struggle came to nothing, and the contending classes met their common ruin, because of a historical transformation – the "formation of an entirely new organisation of society" – imposed by foreign conquerors.[266] But this eventuality is obviously tacitly ruled out in the case of capitalism, presumably for the obvious reason that the technological superiority of capitalist societies[267] allowed them to conquer and exploit other societies rather than vice versa. As Hobsbawm observed,

> [.....]. The world of the 1840s was completely dominated by the European powers, political and economic, supplemented by the growing USA. The Opium War of 1839-42 had demonstrated that the only surviving non-European great power, the

---

[266] Marx & Engels, *Manifest der Kommunistischen Partei*, p. 462; *Die deutsche Ideologie*, p. 23-24.

[267] One may add, also *pre*capitalist Western societies (as demonstrated by the conquests in America and Asia in the 16th century). But the specifically capitalist drive for technological development obviously increased this military superiority.

Chinese Empire, was helpless in the face of Western military and economic aggression. Nothing, it seemed, could henceforth stand in the way of a few Western gunboats and regiments bringing with them trade and Bibles.[268]

In *Die deutsche Ideologie*, more specifically, in an ironic comment on Max Stirner, the British bombardments and the steamships and shrapnel-bombs unfamiliar to the Chinese are mentioned.[269]

The primary, first-hand evidence of Marx' (and Engels') opinion about the inevitability or non-inevitability of the transition from capitalism to socialism and eventually classless communist society is Marx' (and Engels') own words about it, and they are unequivocal and consistent: this transformation is inevitable. So, the question whether Meikle attributes another opinion to them or not is in effect irrelevant: *if* he does, he is wrong; and if anybody else concludes from Meikle's book or books that Marx and Engels only considered the transformation a mere potentiality, they are wrong, whether or not they interpret Meikle correctly.

This may lead to a more general consideration not necessarily relevant to Meikle. Anderson has observed that, "All the main theoretical systems of Western Marxism [.....] had recourse to pre-Marxist philosophies – to legitimate, explicate or supplement the philosophy of Marx himself" – a

---

[268] Hobsbawm, *The Age of Revolution*, p. 355.
[269] Marx & Engels, *Die deutsche Ideologie*, p. 149-150. Cf. Marx, *Das Kapital*, 1, p. 421 (note 133 (where he mordantly describes the abuse of opium in English industrial areas as the revenge of India and China on England; his condemnation of the atrocities and exploitation of colonialism is unmistakable)), p. 779-781. As Marx observes (p. 779), "Violence is the midwife of every old society which is pregnant with a new one. It is itself an economic potency."

"compulsive return behind Marx in quest of a prior vantage-point from which to interpret the meaning of Marx's work itself"[270] which must, while it is neither meaningless nor illegitimate, be practiced with some care. Firstly, the primary evidence of such influence must, again, be found in Marx' texts, neither simply taken for granted or "demonstrated" in the circular movement of reading the philosophy in question into Marx' texts whether this is the most plausible – or even necessary – way to make sense of them or not.

Secondly, Marx and Engels were, after all, themselves thinkers of some stature, and the demonstration that they were influenced by philosopher X, economist Y or natural scientist Z does not mean that we can reduce them to X, Y or Z without more ado – such as examining their texts to establish *how* they themselves interpreted X, Y and Z, and to which extent they accepted, or did not accept, their approaches, concepts and arguments. That is, we cannot merely *assume* that their texts should be read to agree with X, Y or Z at every point; the reality and extent of such agreement must, on the contrary, be tested *by* their texts, read in the way which makes the best sense of them individually and together, with due respect for theoretical development over time.

The failure to observe this principle has been criticised by Timpanaro in the course of a critique of Althusserian Marxism, but referring to a more general trend:

> [.....]. Worse still from a methodological standpoint, structuralist Marxism has exasperated the tendency (already present in a good deal of twentieth-century Marxism) to represent modifications and additions to Marx's thought as 'interpretations' or 'readings' of Marx's texts. *Reading Capital:* there is already a gross

---

[270] Anderson, *Considerations on Western Marxism*, p. 59.

misrepresentation in the title. A *reading*, which once indicated the most respectful and discerning treatment of a text, has become a highly suspect term since Althusser conjured up his 'symptomatic reading' or theoretical forcing of texts. This is an operation which (however changed the setting) takes us back to the worst Italian neo-idealism of the early twentieth century. Then every reading represented a re-creation of the text; in other words, those neo-idealists distorted in a subjectivist direction a serious question, the 'contemporaneity' of the past, which requires a preliminary *objective*, historico-philological interpretation, if it is to be dealt with in a responsible fashion.[271]

So, to draw the general conclusion from these considerations: the primary, first-hand source to what Marx thought is the corpus of his texts,[272] and the dangers of reading these texts

---

[271] Timpanaro, p. 194. Cf. Evans, p. 115: "But surely the past does impose its reality through the sources in a basic way. At the most elementary level, one cannot simply read into documents words that are not there." And p. 120-121: "If a letter from an industrialist says that he does not want any crystallization of the bourgeois right and the Nazis, then no amount of theorizing will alter that fact, and there is no way round it." And in the same way, obviously, if Marx and Engels state that the fall of the bourgeoisie and the victory of the proletariat are equally inevitable, and Marx states that, "Concentration of the means of production and socialization of labour at last reach a point where they become incompatible with their capitalist integument. This integument is burst asunder. The knell of capitalist private property sounds. The expropriators are expropriated" (Marx, *Das Kapital*, 1, p. 791), not as a mere postulate, but in conclusion to his very analysis of capitalism, there is no way round that either.
[272] See Draper, *Karl Marx's Theory of Revolution*, vol. II, p. 3-4 for a categorisation of the writings and documents belonging to this corpus according to their reliability (quoted p. 199-201 below).

through the prisms of other thinkers' ideas[273] – in effect, "decoding" them by using the ideas of other thinkers as the key – should be obvious.[274] If nothing in the texts themselves suggests that Marx should, for example, be understood to think of the transition from capitalism to socialism and eventually classless communist society as merely a potentiality in the Aristotelian sense rather than as an inevitability even when he does in actual fact verbatim describe it as inevitable, then the suggestion that he considered it a mere potentiality (because influenced by Aristotle) must be rejected as implausible because uncorroborated (and indeed gainsaid) by the relevant textual evidence.

---

[273] Cf. Avineri, p. 124-125: "Moses Hess admits that he was deeply influenced by Cieszkowski, and his treatment of *praxis* is so reminiscent of Marx that a claim has recently been made that one cannot fully grasp Marx without recourse to Cieszkowski." (Reference to N. Lobkowicz, "Eschatology and the Young Hegelians", *Review of Politics*, no. 3, July 1963, p. 437).

[274] It would seem to be a legitimate way of reading only when demonstrably making an otherwise unintelligible point in the text intelligible (in the given context).

6. On *Experience and Historical Materialism.*

a.

As a kind of appendix to the above comments on *Structure, Agency and Theory*, it seems reasonable to make some on two points in the Postscript to *Experience and Historical Materialism* which are likely to be considered controversial. The first one is the quotation from Thompson, on p. 289-290, about the "lumpen-intelligentsia" as, according to Thompson, the social basis of Althusserianism,[275] and, as it is suggested in the Postscript, now of the discourse-analytical, postmodernist approach of Laclau & Mouffe and Jenkins. Patrick Finney's piece "Keith Jenkins and the heroic age of British postmodern theory" confirms, even by its very title, that the sense of being part of a new wave, (or, in Thompson's words, an *imaginary* revolutionary psycho-drama), has very likely blunted the critical faculties of those involved:

> [.....]. The later 1990s were consequently a period of titanic struggles as partisans of 'postmodernism' and 'mainstream' counter-insurgents slugged it out in conference halls and seminar rooms, on the burgeoning web and in the pages of learned journals, books and the media.

> These exchanges, it will be recalled, were often impatient and ill-tempered. Accusations of bad faith, misrepresentation, stupidity and malign intent were freely-exchanged. With hindsight, this or that polemical statement might seem unwarranted or excessively exuberant, but they were conditioned by the sense that this was an unwonted period of ferment in which really momentous things were at stake, ideologically and professionally. Of course, every generation succumbs

---

[275] Thompson, *The Poverty of Theory and Other Essays*, p. 3.

to the solipsistic illusion that its own formative moments just are world-historical ones of decisive contestation, but this genuinely was a time of energising excitement when it seemed as if a profound transformation of the discipline might be in the offing. Participating in the birth of this journal, even as a relatively junior player, served for me to reinforce this sense of bracing possibility, and also engendered a comforting sense of belonging to a particular tribe with its own distinctive ethos and values. At a time when British politics appeared to be dissolving into a morass of neoliberal consensualism after the triumph of Tony Blair and New Labour, this alignment also offered a professional means to keep alive a sense of radical endeavour and oppositional politics. So this particular personal investment involved a complex amalgam of intellect, temperament, affect and circumstance.[276]

It is not, of course, argued that this, as expressed in the passage in Thompson, in *Experience and Historical Materialism*, or by Finney himself, is the whole explanation. In fact, a wider social and historical context is suggested in the Postscript.[277] But Finney's words do seem to corroborate that the excitement of feeling a part of a new wave at least goes *some* way to explain the postmodernist trend.

The other point likely to be controversial is the following passage:

> It is important to make very clear what is argued and what is not argued here: Laclau & Mouffe advocate

---

[276] Finney, Patrick: "Keith Jenkins and the heroic age of British postmodern theory", Department of International Politics, Aberystwyth University, UK, Draft Version, p. 8. Published in *Rethinking History*, 17 (2), 2013, 172-191.

[277] *Experience and Historical Materialism*, p. 292-293.

anti-capitalism and radical democracy; Jenkins advocates historiography which may make emancipatory differences within the present. There is no basis for suggesting that they are not sincere. But when told that the "truth" about the being of things depends on the way we classify them, we will do well to remember that within Nazism, a certain way of classifying human beings was current: coolie or fellah races, parasitic races, master and warrior races. And if the "truth" about the being of objects is constituted within the specific theoretical and discursive context, how could Laclau & Mouffe argue that that classification is more *or less* true than any other, for example one suggesting a fundamental likeness of human beings and the irrelevance of the concept of race? And as for Jenkins' suggestion that we cannot know the past, Evans has pointed out that, "Total relativism provides no objective criteria by which fascist or racist views of history can be falsified."[278]

By some readers, this might well be considered an unfair slur on – and coupling of – Laclau & Mouffe on the one hand and Jenkins on the other. In the first place, however, there is no suggestion that either Laclau & Mouffe or Jenkins sympathise with Nazism in any way: it is a matter of the logical implications of their arguments, not their subjective views. Secondly, influence of Laclau & Mouffe on Jenkins, and the position of "total relativism" shared by Laclau and Jenkins, is confirmed by the latter's own words. In *At the Limits of History*, Jenkins offers the following short piece of intellectual autobiography:

---

[278] *Experience and Historical Materialism*, p. 302-303. References to Hofer, p. 32-33, and Evans, p. 239 and ch. 8, III, passim.

In the 1980s I was becoming an adherent of the radical politics and political theory of Ernesto Laclau, out of which a form of 'discursive Marxism' or 'post-Marxism', a Marxism influenced not least by Jacques Derrida and which had jettisoned the notion of historical inevitability whilst retaining key elements of Marxist method and political commitment. My reading of various texts by Paul Hirst and Barry Hindess (not least their *Pre-Capitalist Modes of Production* (1975)), wherein Marxist history had also been rejected, also influenced my move towards post-Marxism, whilst I had also become familiar with the 'cultural studies' and literary theory of Tony Bennett. In 1990 Bennett published his book, *Outside Literature*, in which, in chapters 2 and 3, he rejected Marxist history as teleology but kept a form of historical knowledge which I didn't think he needed to. And so I wrote this paper which was both respectful of Bennett yet critical of him insofar as I didn't think he took the rejection of history to its logical conclusions. Hindess and Hirst did do that, however, and I found their argument both logical – they indeed took their reasoning to its logical conclusion – and convincing. So in this paper I worked Bennett, Laclau, Hindess and Hirst together vis-à-vis my then embryonic notion that we were coming to a certain 'end of history' ... and that this was (probably) a good thing.[279]

This link between Laclau and Mouffe on the one hand and Jenkins on the other is confirmed by the fact that the same passage in Laclau is quoted three times in *At the Limits of History*.[280] In his reply to Zagorin, Jenkins states that,

[279] Jenkins, *At the Limits of History*, p. 22.
[280] Jenkins, *At the Limits of History*, p. 103, p. 241, p. 260; cf. p. 16, p. 25-26, p. 60, p. 107, p. 217-218, p. 224, p. 234, p. 249, p. 267.

[.....] it is this point – that we are all antifoundationalists now – that Zagorin just cannot get. This is illustrated when he plays what I have already referred to as an apparent trump card: that the "skepticism" and relativism postmodernists champion undercuts – if only they knew it – their own positions. But of course they do know it. And they don't care. Because it doesn't matter. For what worries Zagorin – that without foundations you are too weak to rebuff or refute foundational opponents – misses the point that there aren't any credible foundational opponents around any more. Postmodernists are not weak because they have no foundations because nobody has foundations; we are all relativists now, all postmodern now. Accordingly, it is at this point that we arguably reach not only the end of history but the end of ethics too (in the sense that philosophy could ostensibly ground the ethical code) and emerge foundationally naked into the world of the politics of hegemony. Ernesto Laclau has seen this more clearly than most:

> The metaphysical [logocentric] discourse of the West is coming to an end, and philosophy in its twilight has performed a last service for us in the deconstruction of its own terrain. Let us think, for instance, of Derrida's undecidables. Once undecidability has reached the ground itself – once the organisation of a certain camp is governed by a hegemonic decision – hegemonic because it is not objectively determined, because different decisions were also possible – the realm of philosophy comes to an end and the realm of politics begins. This realm will be inhabited by a different type of discourse ...

which ... constructs the world on the "grounds" of a radical undecidability.[281]

This, one may argue, marks the ultimate terminus and bankruptcy of postmodern-style hegemonic politics: if there are no foundations, then what is left to recommend any politics rather than any alternative one, and what is left to decide what politics is or becomes hegemonic other than *either* purely arbitrary choices[282] - *or* the sheer power to force and/or manipulate?[283] *This*, then, is where postmodernist "emancipatory" politics ends – a rather far cry indeed from Engels' words about human agents becoming the masters of their own fate and social organisation in "the kingdom of freedom".[284]

---

[281] Jenkins, *At the Limits of History*, p. 103 (quoting from Laclau, *Emancipations* (London, Verso, 1996), p. 123).

[282] Cf. Lakatos on "the 'scientific sceptic's dilemma'", p. 115 (note 2)).

[283] Cf. Bertramsen, Frølund Thomsen & Torfing, p. 28: "The presence of undecidable moments within the field of the social effectively prevents a rational deduction of means from ends. Since consensus is never an outcome of a series of logical transitions, it must necessarily take the form of an ultimately *arbitrary decision* (Laclau, 1990). In other words, consensus is reached through decisions which have no firm foundation. This means that the process of coming into agreement always involves *persuasion*. The different forms of persuasion describe a continuum ranging from the deployment of both instrumental and noninstrumental forms of *rationality*, through the exercise of *authority* invoking the construction of possible points of identification, to the mobilization of different means of *enforcement*." Significantly, they go on to state that, "The formation of consensus through persuasion is further discussed by Thomas Kuhn who explains the transition from one scientific paradigm to another in terms of a process of *conversion*." (p. 28-29, referring to Kuhn, ch. X). The reference to Laclau is to *New Reflections on the Revolution of Our Time*, London, Verso, 1990.

[284] Engels, *Anti-Dühring*, p. 335-336 (*MEW*, 20, p. 264).

In the first place, Laclau's notions of hegemonic decision not objectively determined and a type of discourse constructing the world on the "grounds" of a radical undecidability demonstrates the point made in *Experience and Historical Materialism* that the consequence of his and Mouffe's *de facto* relativism is that their idea of the "possibility of reasoning politically and of preferring, for a variety of reasons, certain political positions to others" in spite of "the contingent and radically open character" of all the values of a radically democratic society[285] makes no sense when the concept of "truth" has been rendered meaningless by the insistence that every discursive and theoretical context constitutes its own "truth", and the idea of a truth outside all context is simply nonsensical,[286] so that rational argument is substituted by the "truths" defined in the closed circles of whatever discursive contexts people choose, with no common ground between them.[287] The words of Laclau quoted by Jenkins seem to be nothing but the logical implication of Laclau & Mouffe's position in *Hegemony and Socialist Strategy* and "Post-Marxism without Apologies": that no discourse is any more well-founded or true than any other if there is no being of things except that given to them by the given specific discursive and theoretical context, and no such context can be supported by reference to any extradiscursive being or reality.[288]

---

[285] Laclau & Mouffe, "Post-Marxism without Apologies", p. 102.

[286] Laclau & Mouffe, "Post-Marxism without Apologies", p. 85-86.

[287] *Experience and Historical Materialism*, p. 259-260; cf. Geras, "Post-Marxism?", p. 67 (quoted ibid.).

[288] Cf. Laclau & Mouffe, *Hegemony and Socialist Strategy*, p. 115, where they state that "all 'experience' depends on precise discursive conditions of possibility", and their statement in "Post-Marxism without Apologies", p. 91, that nothing follows from the existence of objects, which is the only (and vacuous) extradiscursive reality they were willing to accept.

It is probably worthwhile to spell out (again) precisely why this relativist position is self-defeating: *either* it implies its own relative truth, thus being open to Boghossian's critique quoted by Evans:

> If a claim and its opposite can be equally true provided that there is some perspective relative to which each is true, then, since there is a perspective – realism – relative to which it's true that a claim and its opposite cannot both be true, postmodernism would have to admit that it itself is just as true as its opposite, realism. But postmodernism cannot afford to admit that; presumably, its whole point is that realism is false. Thus, we see that the very statement of postmodernism, construed as a view about truth, undermines itself; facts about truth independent of particular perspectives are presupposed by the view itself.[289]

Or the relativist is guilty of the God's Eye View fallacy, implicitly assuming that all positions are relative, depending as they are on the specific theoretical and discursive context within which they are constituted – *except* this assumption itself on the part of the relativist, who thus tacitly assumes to be making his or her argument about the positions of everybody else from a vantage point above or beyond the relative world and the theoretical and discursive contexts within which others are caught – thus implicitly subverting his or her argument that the "truth" about the being of objects is constituted within such a context, and the idea of a truth outside all context is simply nonsensical, because there is nothing beyond such contexts except the vacuous existence of objects from which nothing follows.

---

[289] Evans, p. 220, quoting from Paul Boghossian, "What the Sokal Hoax ought to teach us", *Times Literary Supplement*, 13 December 1996, p. 15.

Thus, when recommending "radical undecidability" Laclau implicitly recognises the invalidity of his and Mouffe's argument why their position in *Hegemony and Socialist Strategy* has *not* eliminated any possible basis of preferring one type of politics to another:

> [.....] Everything depends on what we understand by 'foundation'. If it is a question of a foundation that enables us to decide with apodictic certainty that one type of society is better than another, the answer is no, there cannot be such a foundation. However, it does not follow that there is no possibility of reasoning politically and of preferring, for a variety of reasons, certain political positions to others. (It is comical that a stern critic of 'either/or' solutions such as Geras confronts us with exactly this type of alternative) Even if we cannot decide algorithmically about many things, this does not mean that we are confined to total nihilism, since we can reason about the *verisimilitude* of the available alternatives. [.....] An argument founded on the apodicticity of the conclusion is an argument which admits neither discussion nor any plurality of viewpoints; on the other hand, an argument which tries to found itself on the verisimilitude of its conclusions, is essentially pluralist, because it needs to make reference to other arguments and, since the process is essentially open, these can always be contested and refuted. The logic of verisimilitude is, in this sense, essentially *public and democratic*. Thus, the first condition of a radically democratic society is to accept the contingent and radically open character of all its values – and in that sense, to abandon the aspiration to a single foundation.[290]

---

[290] Laclau & Mouffe, "Post-Marxism without Apologies", p. 102.

That argument was made by way of an answer to Geras, who had argued that,

> [.....] a pre-discursive reality and an extra-theoretical objectivity form the irreplaceable basis of all rational enquiry, as well as the condition of meaningful communication across and between differing viewpoints. This foundation once removed, one simply slides into a bottomless, relativist gloom, in which opposed discourses or paradigms are left with no common reference point, uselessly trading blows.[291]

In his later rejoinder to them, he made the following observation which pointed out the paradox implicit in the relativist position noted above:

> [.....]. Laclau and Mouffe 'democratically' cut *everybody* off from access to what could meaningfully be called either truth or objectivity – with the single exception, dear to all relativists, of themselves. Overtly denying that there is any being-as-such, any in-itself, in terms of which competing discourses might be adjudicated, they install somewhere out of sight a secret tribunal of truth, mysterious in its ways, which allows *them* to judge here: as 'essentialist', hence *wrong about the nature of the world*; as economist, thus unable to understand the *reality* of the social; as determinist, therefore misconstruing history's *actual* openness, etc.; which allows them to employ a language of external reference, of objectivity, of truth (saying not 'this is how we like to look at it', but 'this is how it *is*, here is what *happened*, *these* are the developments') to tell us what is really what; which allows them that long, that tireless, that never-ending 'this is how it is' with which the relativist

---

[291] Geras, "Post-Marxism?", p. 67.

tells you why you cannot say 'this is how it is', so sending rational knowledge and consistency to the devil.[292]

The relevance of this critique is confirmed by Laclau's arrival at what may be called the logical implication or terminal point of the relativism inherent in his and Mouffe's discourse-analytical position: radical undecidability. Unfortunately, neither the self-contradictory nature of that position, nor the vacuity in terms of ethical and political implications, is overcome.

The fundamental mistake at the bottom of this dead-end is that "existence" is evacuated of any real content, and any "truth" about the "being" of things reduced to an effect of some specific theoretical and discursive context, so that Laclau & Mouffe are able to state, in all earnest, that,

> [.....] it would absurd to ask oneself if, outside all scientific theory, atomic structure is the true 'being' of matter – the answer will be that atomic theory is a way we have of classifying certain objects, but that these are open to different forms of conceptualization that may emerge in the future.[293]

Precisely *because* our practice, our material relation to our material – and immaterial – reality, our experiences and responses, are inevitably mediated by and bound up with *language*, *speech* (whether in the narrow sense or including the written word); because we are "suspended in language", the ways in which we signify and articulate our "lived" reality,

---

[292] Geras, "Ex-Marxism Without Substance", p. 59-60.
[293] Laclau & Mouffe, "Post-Marxism without Apologies", p. 85-86. The absurdity of this postulate may merely be noted: if matter is assumed to exist prior to human beings (cf. ibid. p. 84 on stones), then it must logically be assumed to have had *either* an atomic *or* a non-atomic structure – independently of any theoretical and discursive context.

including material reality, *cannot* be arbitrary. As we are biological beings, with irreducible biological needs and capabilities, part ourselves of the *material* world, that world imposes limits and rules on the ways in which we use language, because we must use language, communicate, in non-arbitrary ways in order to *handle* our "lived" reality, including, as something pivotal and determinant, our own material (physical) survival and reproduction. Experience and language are not articulated according to whim, reality *forces* us to think and communicate and act in certain ways – on penalty of our own extinction.[294]

This is not less real because some areas of abstract theory allow us to play around with (concepts of) language and everything else constituting texts that may be read in an infinite variety of ways: *as long as* the distance from any material practice is kept, such irresponsibility has no material consequences, although those practicing it actually have to keep certain rules of language to be understood – and *are* in fact able to communicate determinable statements insofar as they do so. As Anderson has observed, "[.....], utterance has no material constraint whatever: words are free, in the double sense of the term. They cost nothing to produce, and can be multiplied and manipulated at will, within the laws of meaning."[295]

In contrast to this, we are all, in our normal everyday existence, experiencing the pertinence of Zinkernagel's first rule of language: "We must not use names of ordinary things and expressions of action independently of each other."[296] It is a

---

[294] Cf. Favrholdt, p. 350, p. 357 ff.

[295] Anderson, *In the Tracks of Historical Materialism*, p. 44; he continues by noting that, "All other major social practices are subject to the laws of natural *scarcity*: persons, goods or powers cannot be generated *ad libitum* and *ad infinitum*." (ibid.).

[296] Zinkernagel, p. 51, p. 103.

trivial fact that, for example, "Before we move an inkstand, we cannot move our hand across the spot on the table-top on which the inkstand is, without moving the inkstand", and cannot move our hand through the table-top.[297] So trivial, indeed, that Laclau & Mouffe seem to be able to forget it. As witness the example of a "language game" they quote from Wittgenstein in *Hegemony and Socialist Strategy*, and the comments on it in *Experience and Historical Materialism*:

> [.....] 'A is building with building-stones: there are blocks, pillars, slabs, and beams. B has to pass the stones, and that in the order in which A needs them. For this purpose they use a language consisting of the words "block", "pillar", "slab", "beam". A calls them out; B brings the stone which he has learnt to bring at such and such a call.' The conclusion is inevitable: 'I shall also call the whole, consisting of language and the actions into which it is woven, the "language game".' It is evident that the very material properties of objects are part of what Wittgenstein calls language game, which is an example of what we have called discourse.[298]

It is obvious how the second and the third postulate are indeed interrelated and interdependent: to such a degree that the critique actually works on both of them: while the "language game" in question does effect a material change, the construction of a building from a variety of elements, it is not independent of the material properties of the blocks, pillars, slabs and beams they use, such as their size, shape, weight, and brittleness; in fact one may legitimately assume that

---

[297] Zinkernagel, p. 63, p. 66.
[298] Laclau & Mouffe, *Hegemony and Socialist Strategy*, p. 108.

those properties are determinants of what A and B can do, and how, in order to construct the specific building they make, or indeed any building. And that they cannot materially change those properties except by working materially on the stones, and that in ways likewise depending on the structure and hardness (and given size and shape and weight) of them. In other words, the extra-discursive properties of the stones will be conditioning the "language game", and the real difference between material and immaterial discourses cannot be denied.[299]

Some may likewise fail to realise the implications of Laclau & Mouffe's argument there and on "existence" and "being",[300] simply because of their outlandishness. Their argument about the being of things depending on how we relate to them[301] might, indeed, be read as a concession to the kind of argument about practical, material relationship/interaction with the material world made above. The point of the latter argument is, however, precisely that we cannot, because of the irreducible pre- or extradiscursive reality of the material world, relate to it (in a practical, material sense) in *arbitrary* ways. We cannot, for example, use a mountain as a projectile or a hammer as we might do with a stone.[302] It should be unnecessary to go through the argument on this in *Structure, Agency and Theory* and *Experience and Historical Materialism*, but those who refuse to accept that Laclau & Mouffe are in effect arguing that things are what they are discursively articulated as being, should consider the following passages:

---

[299] *Experience and Historical Materialism*, p. 195-196.
[300] Laclau & Mouffe, "Post-Marxism without Apologies", p. 82 ff. Cf. the fourth essay in *Experience and Historical Materialism* and Structure, Agency and Theory, Part Two, ch. 4.
[301] Laclau & Mouffe, "Post-Marxism without Apologies", p. 82-86.
[302] Laclau & Mouffe, "Post-Marxism without Apologies", p. 84-85.

[.....] even if we assume that there is a strict equation between the social and the discursive, what can we say about the natural world, about the facts of physics, biology or astronomy that are not apparently integrated in meaningful totalities constructed by men? The answer is that natural facts are also discursive facts. And they are so for the simple reason that the idea of nature is not something that is already there, to be read from the appearances of things, but is itself the result of a slow and complex historical and social construction. To call something a natural object is a way of conceiving it that depends upon a classificatory system. Again, this does not put into question that this entity which we call stone exists, in the sense of being present here and now, independently of my will; nevertheless the fact of its being a stone depends on a way of classifying objects that is historical and contingent. If there were no human beings on earth, those objects that we call stones would be there nonetheless; but they would not be 'stones', because there would be neither mineralogy nor a language capable of classifying them and distinguishing them from other objects.[303]

Does this merely mean that without human beings there would be nobody to distinguish this specific kind of objects from others, while their material properties are the same with or without such classification? The following quotation should prove that this is not the case:

[.....]. As we have seen, however, outside of any discursive context objects *do not have* being; they have only *existence*. The accusation of the 'anti-relativist' is, therefore, meaningless, since it presupposes that there is a *being* of things as such, which the relativist is either

---

[303] Laclau & Mouffe, "Post-Marxism without Apologies", p. 83-84.

indifferent to or proclaims to be inaccessible. But, as we have argued, things only have being within a certain discursive configuration, or 'language game', as Wittgenstein would call it. It would be absurd, of course, to ask oneself today if 'being a projectile' is part of the true being of the stone (although the question would have some legitimacy within Platonic metaphysics); the answer, obviously, would be: it depends on the way we use stones. For the same reason it would be absurd to ask oneself if, outside all scientific theory, atomic structure is the 'true being' of matter – the answer will be that atomic theory is a way we have of classifying certain objects, but that these are open to different forms of conceptualization that may emerge in the future. In other words, the 'truth', factual or otherwise, about the being of objects is constituted within a theoretical and discursive context, and the idea of a truth outside all context is simply nonsensical.[304]

As observed in *Experience and Historical Materialism*,

> [.....], if this means anything, it means that, like Kuhn's paradigms, every such theoretical and discursive context constitutes it own "'truth" about, or being of, things, and that such contexts are, like Kuhn's paradigms, incommensurable, because extra-discursive reality has no *being* but only *existence*, and "nothing follows from this existence."[305]

Moreover, this is confirmed by Laclau & Mouffe's assertion that, "Human beings socially construct their world, and it is

---

[304] Laclau & Mouffe, "Post-Marxism without Apologies", p. 85-86.
[305] *Experience and Historical Materialism*, p. 192, quoting Laclau & Mouffe, "Post-Marxism without Apologies", 91.

through this construction – always precarious and incomplete – that they give to a thing *its being*."[306]

It is thus perfectly true that, in Geras' words, "Existence has been emptied of all content to the benefit of being-discourse. It is easy to see why relativism could seem like 'a false problem' from within this perspective. Existence, so emptied, can be no external control for different versions of being, and the hope of any such control is misguided."[307]

If the last two passages quoted from Laclau & Mouffe are not to that effect, then what *can* they mean? As for the "external control", the following passage in Favrholdt was quoted in *Experience and Historical Materialism*:

> [.....] most of the experiments on which quantum mechanics is based would contain hidden errors[.] The wave-particle dualism would be wrong, and all the equations that are used a hundred per cent successfully when designing electron microscopes, transistors, laser-light equipment, television sets, nuclear power stations etc. would presumably be incorrect. It would be inconceivable how this modern technology could have been developed. Such an outcome of the experiment would not have demonstrated that quantum mechanics was inadequate, but that it was self-contradictory, and so far self-contradictory theories have never been of practical use.[308]

b.

As noted in *Experience and Historical Materialism*,

---

[306] Laclau & Mouffe, "Post-Marxism without Apologies", p. 89.
[307] Geras, "Ex-Marxism Without Substance", p. 55-56.
[308] Favrholdt, p. 148, *Experience and Historical Materialism*, p. 270. Cf. Thompson, p. 8-9, quoted in *Experience and Historical Materialism*, p. 269-270.

[.....]. If it were true that every source can be subjected to several, even "endless", interpretations, if readings of texts are, logically, infinite, then it makes no sense for Jenkins to quote Foucault quoting Borges, or Hayden White or anyone else, or to argue his point to persuade readers, nor would it make any sense for historians to write their shifting, problematic discourses which are subject to a logically infinite series of uses and abuses, as readers will read them in an infinite variety of ways anyway – and all human communication and life would break down completely. By its very existence, Jenkins' text gives itself the lie on this point.[309]

Finally, having turned once again to Jenkins, it may be noted in passing that his claims that, "we are all antifoundationalists now", that, "we are all relativists now, all postmodern now"[310] should probably not be taken at their face value, and are in any case gainsaid by the critique of postmodernism offered by Evans, Boghossian, Sokal, Zagorin, Coleman, McIntyre and others, some of whom Jenkins himself has in fact counterattacked; so, who are the "we" ostensibly all postmodern relativists and antifoundationalists? Not everyone with an opinion about postmodernism, certainly.

But we may take it that Jenkins does consider that Lyotard's argument on the *differend* is foundationless/does not constitute a foundation for any politics or ethics,[311] partly because he would otherwise contradict his own insistence that "nobody has foundations",[312] and partly because he actually states that,

---

[309] *Experience and Historical Materialism*, p. 241-242.
[310] Jenkins, *At the Limits of History*, p. 103.
[311] Jenkins, *At the Limits of History*, p. 169-187, p. 197-202, p. 297-300.
[312] Jenkins, *At the Limits of History*, p. 103.

[.....]. To be sure there is a sense in which, in advocating decisionism, I may seem to be contradicting myself by drawing from this fact, this 'is' (this decisionism) a value, an ought (that is, we *ought* to embrace this decisionism). And maybe on the surface of things I am. But I'm *not* drawing this conclusion because it is entailed, but because I just like this way of reading things and think maybe I can defend it: I know my decision to do so is ungrounded. And I am comfortable with this because some of the theorists I admire most – Foucault, Lyotard, Rorty, Butler, Baudrillard, Badiou, Derrida – are ethical to their very 'core' without that 'core' being founded in anything other than an ethico-political preference. There is no time here to go into detail as to how Lyotard *et al.* are highly 'ethical' on the basis of nothing other than, I think, a bottom-line relativism.[313]

So, according to Jenkins, whatever "ethical" decisions these theorists make, they are foundationless and there is no ground on which to discuss them rationally: one may adopt or reject their positions just as one pleases. But if we have to accept such "bottom-line relativism", then the Nazi's way of classifying human beings as belonging to coolie or fellah races, parasitic races and master and warrior races is neither less, nor more, true than any other classification, or rejection of classifications. And if the Nazi likes that classification, and the conception of the parasitic races as inherent foes of other human beings, better than the argument that such a classification is unfounded, and that more human beings will feel better off in a society in which all human beings are equal and able to consume more or toil less because not exploited,

---

[313] Jenkins, *At the Limits of History*, p. 249.

control their own fate to the greatest degree possible[314] and live in peace with one another, than in one based on inequality, dictatorship and the oppression or extermination of supposedly inferior and dangerous races – well, then that is the end of it: one's position is all a matter of foundationless, that is, arbitrary, decision.

To the philosopher in his or her armchair, the idea of having reached "the end of ethics" may seem liberating in the sense that it allows one to choose one's own norms, or a lack of norms, according to one's whim, without having to argue why. In a *practical* sense, however, this may be less liberating for most people, as anyone, or any group, wanting to adopt a practice of oppressing, exploiting and/or killing off anybody they choose may feel free to do so. Anyone who has seen a bully at work in the schoolyard, or has any knowledge about Nazi or Stalinist terror, or the countless other enormities committed throughout history, should know better than Jenkins – and feel less comfortable about his "bottom-line relativism".

If we accept "bottom-line relativism" and "radical undecidability", then there is no way of arguing that a society in which people are more or less arbitrarily jailed, tortured, killed or worked to death in labour camps, and/or sent to fight in wars of aggression (with the members of other societies as victims of these too) is any worse than one in which there is rule of law, and political issues are decided by peaceful, democratic means, or that non-exploitative relations of production are better than exploitative ones. Keith Jenkins would, presumably, claim that he just happens to like the latter better than the former, and this writer would not be inclined to disbelieve him if he did. The problem with his advocacy of "bottom-line relativism" is that the Holocaust, the Gulag, imperialist

---

[314] Wright, *Classes*, p. 28, p. 36, p. 249.

wars, massacres, genocide and ethnic cleanings and other acts of oppression and exploitation (slavery in its various forms, gender and racist discrimination etcetera) are not mere material for philosophical theorising: they have actually taken place, or still do, with real, flesh-and-blood victims. Jenkins may choose left (or "radical") politics (in some sense) because he just happens to like that best; others may choose politics of oppression and murder because *they* just happen to like *that* best. Whether one or the other gains the upper hand is not, however, a mere matter of preference, it is an exceedingly practical one – literally one of life and death – for those having to bear the consequences of the outcome.

Finally, Jenkins is of course contradicting himself when recommending (or feeling comfortable about) the theorists he admires most because they are "ethical to their very 'core'" – on what criteria, pray, and why is being ethical without any foundation more recommendable or comforting than being unethical (whatever the criteria by which to label anything as that are supposed to be)? If we have reached the end of ethics, what can we *mean* by "ethical" and "unethical", and why is this distinction, or any "ethico-political preference", relevant?

Either everything *is* undecidable, and nothing is better than anything else, and all choices and decisions *are* ungrounded, and the recommendation that we should construct our own history as "the beginning of a general recognition of how things seem to operate" that is emancipating[315] is meaningless – as it was when Jenkins published it in *Re-thinking History* almost a decade before his answer to Zagorin, and two before *At the Limits of History* was published. *Or* some criteria of ethical or unethical (such as freedom versus unfreedom) are, consciously or unconsciously, explicitly or tacitly, assumed.

---

[315] Jenkins, *Re-thinking History*, p. 30-31.

Jenkins contradicts himself, and subverts his own postmodernist position by constantly arguing in a way implying the
truth of some things rather than others, and the higher ethical
value of some things, decisions and actions than others.
Zagorin should be given the final word on this, quoting the
following observation on Jenkins and postmodernism from
his "Rejoinder to a postmodernist":

> [.....]. He justifies his presentation with the oft-heard
> but dubious claim that these philosophers are contin-
> ually misunderstood and misread by their critics.
> Hence he is chiefly concerned to set them and me right
> on our alleged misconceptions. It is amusing, though,
> that in some of his comments he adopts a frequent
> postmodernist and deconstructionist device of fram-
> ing certain epistemic terms in warning quotation
> marks. Thus, he talks of reading postmodernism "'cor-
> rectly,'" reading it "'wrong,'" and reading it "'right'
> [.....], and he complains that a certain remark about
> Derrida is mind-blowingly "'wrong'" [.....]. Are these
> terms supposed to have a different meaning when en-
> closed in quotation marks? Can we read something
> "correctly" but not correctly? And is being "wrong" or
> "right" not the same as being wrong or right? This
> manner of argument is typical of the self-contradic-
> tions of postmodernist theory in purporting to assert
> that it knows something while simultaneously aiming
> to undermine claims to objective knowledge.[316]

---

[316] Zagorin, "Rejoinder to a postmodernist" (*History and Theory*, 39,
2, 2000), quoted from *At the Limits of History*, p. 111. Cf. Evans, p.
277-278. An effective critique of Jenkins is Guy Halsall: "Post-
Modern History: A critique (for students) of Keith Jenkins' Re-
Thinking History" edgyhistorian.blogspot.com/2016/post-mod-
ern-history-critique-for.html.

7. Once Again, the Problem of Reading Marx.

a.

As the problem of reading Marx has been a prominent issue in *Experience and Historical Materialism* and *Structure, Agency and Theory* as well as the critiques of Mau and Meiksins Wood in the present volume, it seems reasonable to treat it a bit more generally in this final essay, thus also gathering up some threads.

One thing which has been criticised in *Experience and Historical Materialism* and *Structure, Agency and Theory* as well as in the first, second and fifth of the preceding essays, is the misleading and often arbitrary ways in which the texts of Marx and Engels have been read and interpreted to evade various unwanted theoretical elements or statements. What should be kept firmly in mind is that the *only* first-hand, primary evidence we have about what Marx and Engels really thought and meant to say are these texts which they have left behind. Hal Draper has drawn up a list of categories of these texts, in descending order of reliability. It may be just as well to quote it in full here:

> 1. Books and major essays that were published under the control of the writer, with the usual opportunity for correction, revision, etc. (Most of Marx's or Engels' major works will come to mind as examples.)
> 2. Articles published under the control of the writer.
> a. Articles composed as political statements, for a political audience, and signed; in short, intended for the purpose they are used for.
> b. Articles in which remarks on issues occur only in passing, often elliptically.
> c. Journalistic articles, written as hack work, perhaps not even signed.

3. Articles published not under the control of the writer. Perhaps the most extreme case is that of *New York Tribune* articles that were rewritten or added to at will by the editors.

4. Unpublished manuscripts.

a. Unfinished or fragmentary, often never reviewed or revised – unfinished for various possible reasons, including dissatisfaction with the work.

b. Finished – but unpublished for various possible reasons, including dissatisfaction.

5. Letters. The circumstances of a letter, including its addressee, must always be taken into account. When writing to Engels, Marx takes much for granted and does not have to phrase his thoughts as they come to the pen in order to avoid ignorant or malicious misinterpretation. Some letters to others are diplomatizing. All letters are timebound: opinions expressed (for example, about people) may change. Letters are prime examples of ad-hoc writings that cannot be usefully quoted until the context is evaluated.

a. Circular letters. These are very like political statements, more like considered articles than casual correspondence.

b. "Educational" letters. Written to strangers in some cases, to party leaders in others, these are written with some conscious effort to set down a view; but even so, without the responsibilities entailed by publication.

c. Intimate letters, where all is "thinking aloud" and no effort is made to avoid possible misunderstandings by a third party. Most of the correspondence between Marx and Engels comes under this head. Very often, general-sounding statements have specific contexts and meanings.

d. Casual or ad-hoc letters, perhaps hastily dashed off, given little or no considerations of any kind.

6. Private notes, notebooks, and workbooks. These were not only not written for publication but were often written in a personal "shorthand" or in a telegraphic and allusive style, intended only for the writer's eyes. The aforementioned *Grundrisse* is an example of a long work in this style; Marx's "Conspectus of Bakunin's Book &c." is a shorter and more fragmentary case.[317]

In *Experience and Historical Materialism*, a list of the errors involved in the examples of misinterpretations dealt with in the second essay in that book was drawn up, leaning on Draper's categorisation of the texts:

1. The failure to distinguish between *more* and *less* finished and reliable texts by Marx and Engels.
2. The failure to base interpretations on the most reliable and relevant texts *as a whole* and consider what interpretation is most consistent with that evidence.
3. Quotation-mongering, that is, quoting utterances from Marx' and Engels' writings out of context in support of interpretations they do not support when read in their context. The interpretation of Marx' and Engels' general views from statements on specific cases and vice versa is a special variety of this error.
4. Confounding the question of *determinism* with that of *fatalism*: as should be abundantly documented above, Marx' and Engels' determinism is based on their expectations in terms of *agency*, the eventual responses and capacities of the working class.
5. The willingness to dismiss explicit but inconvenient utterances in Marx and Engels as a "verbal tribute",

---

[317] Draper, *Karl Marx's Theory of Revolution*, II, *The Politics of Social Classes*, p. 3-4. As argued in *Experience and Historical Materialism*, section d. of the second essay, Draper himself misreads the *Manifesto*.

"rhetorical flourish" or cases of "cheering on the troops".[318]

It will be seen that the misinterpretations in Mau[319] discussed in the first essay above belong to category 1, 3 and 5 on this list. Mau accepts Heinrich's dismissal of a statement in *Capital* which is supported both by the context in which it is made and similar statements in other finished and published texts of Marx and Engels. He interprets the statements in Marx' letter to the editorial board of the *Otechestvenniye Zapiski* and in the drafts of the letter to Zasulich and the letter itself on the historical inevitability of the primitive accumulation in Western Europe as a rejection of inevitable historical transformations *in general*, disregarding assertions of the inevitability of that from capitalism to socialism in *Capital* (such as that dismissed as declamatory by Heinrich, although Marx confirmed it in the letter to the editorial board of the *Otechestvenniye Zapiski*), *Anti-Dühring* and the two first drafts of the letter to Zasulich.

Likewise, he interprets a passage in Marx' *1861-63 Manuscripts* to the effect that Marx only thought of "natural laws" in terms of "the *essential* and *historically specific* determinations of a mode of production, not to the way in which a transhistorical technological drive smashes through the fetters of historical particularities."[320] Thus ignoring the passage by a Russian reviewer who was quoted by Marx as providing an accurate depiction of the dialectical method which he, Marx, used, to the effect that the most important thing for Marx is the law of the transition from one mode of production to another, the necessity of which transition is, according to the reviewer,

---

[318] *Experience and Historical Materialism*, p. 108.
[319] Mau, p. 107-109.
[320] Mau, p. 109.

demonstrated by Marx.[321] And for that matter the section in *Capital* on "the historical tendency of capitalist accumulation" in which it is asserted that the monopoly of capital becomes a fetter upon the mode of production, that the inconsistency between the centralisation of the means of production and the socialisation of labour will reach a point at which they become incompatible with their capitalist integument, which will consequently be burst asunder,[322] like that of individual production was burst asunder when they had turned into fetters on the development of the productive forces.[323]

Just as in the two first drafts of the letter to Zasulich and in *Anti-Dühring*,[324] where the conclusion on the inevitable supersession of capitalism is quoted,[325] it is obvious that it is the conception of the dialectic of forces and relations of production as the motive power of historical development and transformations which is the framework of explanation and prediction here, the conception discernible from the mid-1840s (*Die deutsche Ideologie*), and "achieving its paradigmatic formulation in the preface to the *Contribution to the Critique of Political Economy*".[326] And equally obviously, not just Mau's interpretation of the texts dealt with here, but also his sketch of Marx' intellectual development from the 1860s and on is wrong. There is hardly any reason to pursue the matter further, except by noting that if Mau had argued that Marx and Engels *should* have abandoned the concept of the dialectic of forces and relations production as the motive power of historical development and transformations, accepting that they did not in fact do so, this writer would have no quarrel with that position.

---

[321] Marx, *Das Kapital*, 1, p. 25-27
[322] Marx, *Das Kapital*, 1, p. 791.
[323] Marx, *Das Kapital*, 1, ch. 24.7.
[324] Engels, *Anti-Dühring*, Part III, ch. II, passim.
[325] Engels, *Anti-Dühring*, p. 159-160 (*MEW*, 20, p. 123-124).
[326] Mau, p. 107.

With due respect for their specificity and different degrees of reliability, we may confront one text with another; and we are free to reject whatever we find untenable, or any reading which is demonstrably inconsistent with the texts, or more specifically with the most reliable texts.

What we should not do is to override statements in the most reliable texts by reference to some statement in a less reliable one, unless there are really strong reasons for doing so. Or reject a straightforward reading of statements in reliable texts on the strength of a single one in a text perhaps belonging to a less reliable category. Or dismiss statements embedded in and supported by substantial expositions in the most reliable texts as "cheering on the troops",[327] "merely 'declamatory'"[328] or "some ambiguous formulations".[329] Nor, of course, fail to notice unmistakable statements to the effect that capitalism is bound to be superseded by socialism and eventually classless communist society in a published work as well as drafts of letters.[330]

In the final analysis, we cannot get "behind" the texts of Marx and Engels to find the "real" Marx and Engels; there is no privileged position from which we can read their real thoughts independently of the texts and evaluate and rank the same texts according to their consistency with those thoughts, or exclude this or that statement as something they did not really mean, or read various statements differently from what they seem to mean. Nor can we read their statements in that way – interpreting, for example, "inevitability" as "potentiality" – on the strength of the assumed influence

---

[327] Collier, p. 143.
[328] Mau, p. 107.
[329] Blackledge, p. 46.
[330] Mau, p. 108.

of whatever writer: such influence on them must be readable from their words as they stand, and if we approach their texts on the assumption that they are written in code and can and must be decoded by reading the concepts and views of some other writer into them, our reading is in effect arbitrary. Unless there are strong reasons for believing otherwise, we have to assume that they wrote what they meant and meant what they wrote.

This does not, of course mean that we should not avail ourselves of relevant methods and means of interpreting texts, such as whatever knowledge we have about the meanings of words and concepts at the relevant points in time and space. But whatever interpretation we attempt to make of a given text, it has to make demonstrably (better) sense in their context, and within the limits set by their actual wording.

It is unmistakable from much of the literature on historical materialism published in the last fifty or sixty years that there are many more or less conflicting interpretations of Marx (and Engels). To evaluate them and judge between them, some seriousness in reading the texts is certainly required. And has been demonstrated in *Structure, Agency and Theory* and *Experience and Historical Materialism*, such seriousness has sometimes been lacking.

More specifically, while there are valid reasons for rejecting the conception of the dialectic of forces and relations of production as the motive power of historical development and transformations as untenable, there is no sound textual basis for dismissing it as mere cheering on the troops, etcetera, or asserting that it disappeared entirely from Marx' writings after 1875, or that he explicitly opposed it towards the end of his life. This conception is, on the contrary, firmly embedded in, and informing, key arguments in key texts by Marx (and Engels). And so far, no one has, to the best knowledge of this writer, dug up any cogent evidence that they did not take it seriously.[331] Indeed, considering the part played by the conception of the dialectic of forces and relations of production in *Die deutsche Ideologie*, the *Manifesto*, the Preface to *A Contribution to the Critique of Political Economy*, *Capital* (vol. 1, especially ch. 24.7), *Anti-Dühring* and, for that matter, in the first two drafts of the letter to V. I. Zasulich, the assertion that Marx and Engels did not take it seriously, and/or dropped it after 1875, or that it was a mere matter of cheering on the troops, or merely declamatory, or reducible to a (misreading of) some ambiguous remarks, are too facile.

In other words, this dialectic has to be accepted as a central element of what they meant to communicate, and on which they based their expectations, predictions and strategic reasoning. In itself, the wish to excise it is understandable, as Marx' and Engels' expectations and predictions have not come true, and the conception of the dialectic of forces and relations of production as the motive power of historical development and transformations seems less and less able to make sense of the history of advanced capitalist societies. However, while the dismissal of it as something at best marginal in Marx and Engels (or something nonexistent), or no more than declamations, etcetera, is bad scholarship, it also tends to distract attention from the strategic *gap* in historical materialism left by its excision. If we cannot rely on that dialectic to prompt the working class to accomplish the

---

[331] As pointed out in the fifth essay, the passage about the possibility of class struggles *in the past* ending "either in a revolutionary reconstitution of society at large, or in the common ruin of the contending classes" (Marx & Engels, *Manifest der Kommunistichen Partei*, p. 462; cf. *Die deutsche Ideologie*, p. 23-24 for a plausible answer to the question of its meaning) *cannot* be considered a disclaimer of their assertion of the inevitability of the supersession of capitalism by (socialism and eventually) communism (*Manifest der Kommunistischen Partei*, p. 467-474).

transition to socialism and eventually classless communist society once capitalist relations of production have turned into fetters on the development of the productive forces, let alone to enable it to do so, how is that transition to be successfully brought off?

The question is not whether the capitalist working class has a fundamental, objective interest in that transition, but whether – and how – it may be effectively organised around it, and how the *effectively* collective command of the means, power and outcome of production is to be realised – at a sufficient high level of material production *and* sustainable.

b.

If we consider the fact and place of the conception of the dialectic of forces and relations of production as the motive power of historical development and transformations in Marx' and Engels' historical materialism,[332] the idea of a law of historical development and transformations according to which the transition from one mode of production or type of society to another occurs (or may occur) when a class with (or believing that it has) an interest in (certain actions amounting to) doing away with the existing/dominant relations of production, even if this class may not be positively aware of causing a historical transformation, is not unreasonable.[333]

The assumption that this *will* actually happen whenever – and *only* when – these relations of production have turned into

---

[332] As classically stated by Marx in the Preface to *A Contribution to the Critique of Political Economy*, p. 21-22 (*MEW*, 13, p. 9).

[333] This loose formulation is compatible both with the possibility of the failure of the class in question to cause a transformation, and that of such a transformation being accomplished by invaders conquering the social formation in question (cf. Marx & Engels, *Die deutsche Ideologie*, p. 23-24; *Manifest der Kommunistischen Partei*, p. 462).

fetters on the development of the forces of production is a more problematic one: firstly, it implies that the potentially revolutionary class is aware of its interest in the historical transformation (or the actions amounting to it) *and* possesses the class capacities required to accomplish it; secondly, it tends towards an implicit teleological assumption, with the development of the forces of production as the *telos* of the (pre)history of human society. The second point is, admittedly, a moot one, inasmuch as Marx and Engels explicitly rejected teleological explanations of historical developments.[334] But in effect such teleology is a *logical*, even if not a realised, precondition for considering such transformations inevitable. Or, to be more specific, it is only on teleological assumptions one can take it for granted that,

> [.....]. No social order is ever destroyed before all the productive forces for which it is sufficient have been developed, and new superior relations of production never replace older ones before the material conditions for their existence have matured within the framework of the old society. Mankind thus inevitably sets itself only such tasks as it is able to solve, since closer examination will always show that the problem itself arises only when the material conditions for its solution are already present or at least in the course of formation.[335]

To be sure, that new relations never replace older ones before the material conditions for their existence have come into being is, of course, a truism. But that mankind inevitably sets itself only such tasks as it is able to solve implies a causal link

---

[334] Marx & Engels, *Die heilige Familie*, p. 98, *Die deutsche Ideologie*, p. 45.

[335] Marx, *A Contribution to the Critique of Political Economy*, p. 21 (*MEW*, 13, p. 9).

between relations and forces of production on the one hand and agents' articulation of their experiences of and responses to their "lived reality on the other which it seems hazardous to take for granted.

But Marx was confident that the capitalist working class would be "always increasing in numbers, and disciplined, united, organised by the very mechanism of the capitalist process of production."[336] Engels expressed his confidence that, "Whilst the capitalist mode of production more and more completely transforms the great majority of the population into proletarians, it creates the power which, under penalty of its own destruction, is forced to accomplish this revolution", and that the way to accomplish this revolution: the proletariat seizing political power and turning the means of production in the first instance into state property, would be demonstrated by capitalist development itself.[337] *And* that class divisions, based upon the insufficiency of production, "will be swept away by the complete development of modern productive forces."[338]

The relationship, or interaction, between social circumstances and agency, and that between human intentions and their realisation in the given circumstances would seem to be more complex: did the Russian Bolsheviks, for example, succeed in their strategic endeavours? And what about the isolation of class struggle in advanced capitalist societies? How certain is it that a socialist, and eventually communist, economy can actually *work* at the required level of material (and sustainable!) production? The conception of the dialectic of forces and relations of production as the motive power of

---

[336] Marx, *Das Kapital*, 1, p. 790-791.
[337] Engels, *Anti-Dühring*, p. 332 (*MEW*, 20, p. 261).
[338] Engels, *Anti-Dühring*, p. 334 (*MEW*, 20, p. 263).

historical development and transformations is too simple to take such uncertainties properly into account.

What is argued in *Structure, Agency and Theory* by way of overcoming this weakness of historical materialism is to discard the conception of the dialectic of forces and relations of production as the motive power of historical development and transformations and hence Marx' and Engels' confidence in the inevitability of the transition from capitalism to socialism and eventually classless communist society and consider the interaction between social circumstances and agency as that motive power, with agents' articulation of their experiences of and responses to their "lived" reality as a crucial determinant, and historical development conceived of as an *open-ended* process.

This, then, is the point where, leaving the secondary question of Marx' intellectual development behind and turning to the primary one of what *kind* of process historical development is, this writer and Mau may meet: discarding the conception of the dialectic of forces and relations of production as the motive power of historical development and transformations and agreeing that,

> What drives history is not the immanent and necessary development of the productive forces, but human beings acting within a set of determinate social structures from which certain tendencies arise.[339]

The remaining, and decisive, question is how to *handle* these structures and tendencies.

---

[339] Mau, p. 108.

References.

Addison, Paul: The Road to 1945: *British Politics and the Second World War*. London 1994 [1st edition 1975].

Anderson, Perry: *Considerations on Western Marxism*. London 1976 [2nd impression 1977].

Anderson, Perry: *In the Tracks of Historical Materialism: The Wellek Library Lectures*. London 1983.

Anderson, Perry: *Lineages of the Absolutist State*. London 1979 [1974].

Avineri, Shlomo: *The Social and Political Thought of Karl Marx*. London 1968.

Balibar, Étienne: "Self Criticism: An Answer to Questions from 'Theoretical Practice'" *Theoretical Practice* no 7-8, January 1973.

Baran, Paul A. & Sweezy, Paul M.: *Monopoly Capital. An Essay on the American Economic and Social Order*. Harmondsworth, Middlesex 1977 [1966].

Bertramsen, René Bugge & Frølund Thomsen, Jens Peter & Torfing, Jacob: *State, Economy and Society*. London 1979.

Bohr, Niels: *Atomic Physics and Human Knowledge*. Mineola, New York 2010 [København 19579.

Bosch, Reinout: *Historisk Materialisme: Materialistisk historieteori under postmodernistisk hegemoni*. Frederiksberg 2020.

Carr, E. H.: *What Is History?* Harmondsworth, Middlesex 1964 [London 1961].

Cohen, Gerald Allan: *Karl Marx's Theory of History: a Defence*. Princeton, New Jersey 2009.

Darwin, Charles: *The Origin of Species*. New York 1928 [6th edition 1882 (1st edition 1859)].

Dobb, Maurice: *Studies in the Development of Capitalism*. London 1963 [1st edition 1946].

Draper, Hal: *Karl Marx's Theory of Revolution*. New York – London 1977-1986.

Engels, Friedrich: *Anti-Dühring. Herr Eugen Dühring's Revolution in Science*. London 1975. *MEW*, 20.

Engels, Friedrich: "Engels an Marx in London, 11. oder 12. Dezember 1859" *MEW*, 29.

Esping-Andersen, Gösta: *The Three Worlds of Welfare Capitalism*. Cambridge – Oxford 1990.

Evans, Richard J.: *In Defence of History*. London 2000 [1997].

Favrholdt, David: *Filosoffen Niels Bohr*. København 2009.

Finney, Patrick: "Keith Jenkins and the heroic age of British postmodern Theory". Draft version [published in *Rethinking History*, 17 (2) 2013].

French, A. P. & Kennedy, P. J. (eds.): *Niels Bohr. A Centenary Volume*. Cambridge, Massachusetts – London 1985.

Geras, Norman: "Ex-Marxism Without Substance: Being a Real Reply to Laclau & Mouffe" *New Left Review* no 169, 1988.

Geras, Norman: "Post-Marxism?" *New Left Review* no 163, 1987.

Goodin, Robert E. & Headey, Bruce & Muffels, Ruud & Dirven, Hen-Jan: *The Real Worlds of Welfare Capitalism*. Cambridge 1999.

Gram-Jensen, Ib: *Experience and Historical Materialism: Five Argumentative Essays*. København 2020.

Gram-Jensen, Ib: *Structure, Agency and Theory: Contributions to Historical Materialism and the Analysis of Classes, State and Bourgeois Power in Advanced Capitalist Societies*. Hellerup 2021.

Herferth, Willi: *Sachregister Marx/Engels Werke*. Studien zur Dialektik Köln 1983.

Hexter, J. H.: *Doing History*. Bloomington – London 1971.

Hickey, Stephen: "The Shaping of the German Labour Movement: Miners in the Ruhr" in: Evans, Richard (ed.): *Society and Politics in Wilhelmine Germany*. London 1978.

Hindess, Barry & Hirst, Paul: *Pre-Capitalist Modes of Production*. London 1975.

Hobsbawm, Eric J.: *Age of Extremes. The Short Twentieth Century 1914-1991*. London 1994.

Hobsbawm, Eric J.: *The Age of Revolution 1789-1848*. New York – Toronto – London 1962.

Hofer, Walther: *Der Nationalsozialismus. Dokumente 1933-1945*. Frankfurt am Main 1957.

Jenkins, Keith: *At the Limits of History: Essays on Theory and Practice*. London – New York 2009.

Jenkins, Keith: *Re-thinking History*. London 2003 [1991].

Kuhn, Thomas S.: *The Structure of Scientific Revolutions*. 3rd edition Chicago 1996 [1962].

Laclau, Ernesto: *Politics and Ideology in Marxist Theory. Capitalism – Fascism – Populism*. London 1979 [1977].

Laclau, Ernesto & Mouffe, Chantal: *Hegemony and Socialist Strategy. Towards a Radical Democratic Politics*. London 1985.

Laclau, Ernesto & Mouffe, Chantal: "Post-Marxism without Apologies" *New Left Review* no 166, 1987.

Lakatos, Imre: "Falsification and the Methodology of Scientific Research Programmes" in: Lakatos, Imre & Musgrave, Alan (eds.): *Criticism and the Growth of Knowledge*. Proceedings of the International Colloquium in the Philosophy of Science, London 1965, volume 4 London 1970.

Levine, Andrew & Wright, Erik Olin: "Rationality and Class Struggle" *New Left Review* no 123, 1980.

Marx, Karl: *A Contribution to the Critique of Political Economy*. New York 1970. MEW, 13.

Marx, Karl: ["Brief an die Redaktion der "Otetschestwennyje Sapiski""] *MEW*, 19 [1977 (?)].

Marx, Karl: [Brief an V. I. Sassulitsch, 8. März 1881] *MEW*, 19.

Marx, Karl: ["Entwürfe einer Antwort auf den Brief von V. I. Sassulitsch"] *Mew*, 19.

Marx, Karl: *Das Elend der Philosophie. Antwort auf Proudhons "Philosophie des Elends"*. *MEW*, 4 [Paris-Bruxelles 1847].

Marx, Karl: *Das Kapital. Kritik der Politischen Ökonomie*. MEW, 23-24-25 [1867, 1885, 1894].

Marx, Karl: *Der Bürgerkrieg in Frankreich. Adresse des Generalrats der Internationalen Arbeiter-Association.* Berlin 1981 [London 1871]. *MEW*, 17.

Marx, Karl: "Der Generalrat an den Föderalrat der romanischen Schweiz." *MEW*, 16.

Marx, Karl: *Early Writings.* Harmondsworth, Middlesex 1975.

Marx, Karl: *Grundrisse: Foundations of the Critique of Political Economy (Rough Draft).* London 1993 [1973; 1st edition Moscow 1939, 1941].

Marx, Karl: "Marx an Ferdinand Lasalle in Berlin, 16. Januar 1861" *MEW*, 30.

Marx, Karl: "Marx an Pawel Wassiljewitsch Annenkow in Paris, 28. Dezember [1846]" *MEW*, 4.

Marx, Karl: "Rede auf der Jahresfeier des "People's Paper" am 14. April 1856 in London" *MEW*, 12.

Marx, Karl: *The Eighteenth Brumaire of Louis Bonaparte.* In: *Surveys from Exile* (edited by David Fernbach) New York 1974. *MEW*, 8.

Marx Karl: *Theorien über den Mehrwert. MEW*, 26.1-3.

Marx, Karl: [Vorbemerkung zur franz¨sischen Ausgabe (1880)] in Engels, Friedrich: *Die Entwicklung des Sozialismus von der Utopie zur Wissenschaft. MEW*, 19.

Marx, Karl & Engels, Friedrich: *Die deutsche Ideologie. Kritik der neuesten deutschen Philosophie und ihren Repräsentanten, Feuerbach, B. Bauer und Stirner und des deutschen Sozialismus in seinen verschiedenen Propheten. MEW*, 3.

Marx, Karl & Engels, Friedrich: *Die heilige Familie oder Kritik der kritischen Kritik. Gegen Bruno Bauer und Konsorten. MEW*, 2 [Frankfurt am Main 1845].

Marx, Karl & Engels, Friedrich: *Manifest der Kommunistischen Partei. MEW*, 4 [London 1848].

Mau, Søren: *Mute Compulsion: A Marxist Theory of the Economic Power of Capital.* London – New York 2023.

Meiksins Wood, Ellen: *Democracy Against Capitalism: Renewing Historical Materialism.* London 2016 [Cambridge 1995].

Parkin, Frank: *Marxism and Class Theory: A Bourgeois Critique.* London 1979.

Parsons, Talcott: *The Structure of Social Action.* New York – London 1968 [1937, 1948].

Perry, Matt: *Marxism and History.* Basingstoke, Hampshire 2002.

Poulantzas, Nicos: *Classes in Contemporary Capitalism.* London 1978 [Editions du Seuil 1974].

Poulantzas, Nicos: *Fascism and Dictatorship.* London 1979 [Paris 1970].

Poulantzas, Nicos: *Political Power and Social Classes.* London 1973 [Paris 1968].

Popper, Karl Raimund: *The Poverty of Historicism.* London 1986 [1957].

Przeworski, Adam: *Capitalism and Social Democracy.* Cambridge 1985.

Rigby, Stephen S.: *Marxism and History: A Critical Introduction.* 2nd edition Manchester 1998 [1st edition 1987].

Sørensen, Curt: *Den europæiske deltagelseskrise – stormagtspolitik, massedeltagelse og ideologi i det 20. århundrede.* Frederiksberg 2017.

Sørensen, Curt: *Marxismen og den sociale orden.* Grenå 1976.

Therborn, Göran: "The Rule of Capital and the Rise of Democracy" *New Left Review* no 103, 1977.

Thompson, E. P.: *The Poverty of Theory.* London 1995.

Thompson, E. P.: *The Poverty of Theory and Other Essays.* London 1978.

Timpanaro, Sebastiano: *On Materialism.* London 1975 [1970, 1973].

Wheen, Francis: *Karl Marx.* London 2000 (1st edition London 1999].

Witt-Hansen, Johannes: *Historisk Materialisme.* København 1973.

Wood, Alan W. Wood (ed.): *Marx Selections.* New York – London 1988.

Wright, Erik Olin: *Class, Crisis and the State*. London 1979 [1978].

Wright, Erik Olin: *Classes*. London 1985.

Wright, Erik Olin & Levine, Andrew & Sober, Elliott: *Reconstructing Marxism: Essays on Explanation and the Theory of History*. London 1992.

Zagorin, Perez: "Rejoinder to a postmodernist" in: Jenkins, Keith: *At the Limits of History: Essays on Theory and Practice*. London – New York 2009.

Zinkernagel, Peter: *Conditions for Description*. London 1962.